The Lark

Jean Anouilh

Translated by
Christopher Fry

Samuel French - London
New York - Toronto - Hollywood

86 0062836 7

WIGAN AND LEIGH COLLEGE

Please see page iv for further copyright information.

THE LARK

Presented at The Lyric Theatre, Hammersmith, on the 11th May 1955 with the following cast of characters—

(in the order of speaking)

BEAUCHAMP, Earl of Warwick	*Richard Johnson*
CAUCHON, Bishop of Beauvais	*Laurence Naismith*
JOAN	*Dorothy Tutin*
HER FATHER	*Peter Duguid*
HER MOTHER	*Alexis France*
HER BROTHER	*Barry MacGregor*
THE PROMOTER	*Leo McKern*
THE INQUISITOR	*Michael Goodliffe*
BROTHER LADVENU	*Michael David*
ROBERT DE BEAUDRICOURT, Squire of Vaucouleurs	*David Bird*
BOUDOUSSE, a guard	*Churton Fairman*
AGNES SOREL	*Hazel Penwarden*
THE YOUNG QUEEN	*Catherine Feller*
CHARLES, The Dauphin	*Donald Pleasence*
QUEEN YOLANDE	*Lucienne Hill*
ARCHBISHOP OF RHEIMS	*John Gill*
M. DE LA TREMOUILLE	*Peter Cellier*
PAGE TO THE DAUPHIN	*David Spenser*
CAPTAIN LA HIRE	*George Murcell*
THE HANGMAN	*Gareth Jones*
AN ENGLISH SOLDIER	*Norman Scace*

THREE SOLDIERS

Directed by PETER BROOK

Scenery and costumes based on designs by JEAN-DENIS MALCLÈS

The Play is in two parts

THE LARK

PART I

*A permanent setting with backcloth and wings is used throughout, with
three sections of "fence", three rostrums and some stools which are
moved as directed during the action.*
(See Ground Plans)

When the CURTAIN *rises the rostrums are* LC, *one section of fence is* C,
one section down R *and one section up* R. *There is a stool down* C *and a
stool down* R. *See Ground Plan A.* JOAN *is on the floor* L *of the stool
down* C, *her arms and head resting on the stool.* BROTHER LADVENU
enters up L *and stands behind the fence* C. THE INQUISITOR *enters
down* L *on the rostrum and sits on the top step at the down-stage end.
Joan's* FATHER, MOTHER *and* BROTHER *enter down* R *and stand
behind the fence down* R, MOTHER C *of it, with* FATHER L *of her and*
BROTHER R *of her.* CAUCHON, BISHOP OF BEAUVAIS, *enters* LC. *He
crosses to* C, *has a few words with* LADVENU *then goes down* R.
The PROMOTER *enters up* R *and stands behind the fence up* R. *A*
SOLDIER *enters up* L *and stands up* LC. *Another* SOLDIER *enters up* R
and stands up RC. *Finally,* BEAUCHAMP, EARL OF WARWICK, *enters
up* R *and comes down to* L *of Cauchon. He wears gauntlets and carries
a walking-stick.*

WARWICK. Well, now; is everyone here? (*He removes his gauntlets*) If so, let's have the trial and be done with it. The sooner
she is found guilty and burned the better for all concerned.
CAUCHON. But, my lord, before we do that we have the whole
story to play: Domremy, the Voices, Vaucouleurs, Chinon, the
Coronation.
WARWICK. Theatrical poppycock! You can tell that story to
the children. The beautiful white armour: the fluttering standard:
the gentle and implacable warrior maid. The statues of her can
tell that story, later on, when policies have changed. We might
even put up a statue ourselves in London, though I know at
the moment that sounds wildly improbable: but, in a few
hundred years, perhaps, it might suit His Majesty's Government
for some reason or other. (*He crosses to* L *of Joan*) But, as for now,
I am Beauchamp, Earl of Warwick, and I've got my grubby
little witch lying on the straw in the dungeon at Rouen, and a
fine packet of trouble she has been, and a pretty sum she has cost
us; but the money's been paid, and the next thing is to put her
on trial and burn her.
CAUCHON (*moving* RC) Not immediately. Before we come to that,

there's the whole of her life to go through. It won't take very long, my lord.

WARWICK (*moving down* L) Well, if you insist. An Englishman knows how to wait. You're not expecting, I hope, to let her go through that monstrous coronation again and all those battles— Orleans, Patay, Beaugency? I may as well tell you now, I should find that in appalling taste.

CAUCHON (*smiling*) Put your mind at rest, my lord. There are too few of us here to stage the battles.

WARWICK (*bowing*) Good. (*He moves down* L *and leans against the proscenium arch*)

(CAUCHON *crosses above Joan to the rostrum and sits* C *of the second step*)

CAUCHON. Joan.

(JOAN *looks up*)

You may begin.

JOAN. May I begin wherever I like?

CAUCHON. Yes.

JOAN. I like to remember the beginning: at home, in the fields, when I was still a little girl looking after the sheep, the first time I heard the Voices. (*She pauses*) It is after the evening Angelus. (*She kneels*) I am very small and my hair is still in pigtails. I am sitting in the field, thinking of nothing at all. God is good, and keeps me safe and happy, close to my mother and my father and my brother, in the quiet countryside of Domremy. My big sheep-dog is lying with his head in my lap; and suddenly I feel his body ripple and tremble, and a hand seems to have touched my shoulder, though I know no one has touched me, and the Voice says . . .

SOLDIER (*up* RC) Who is going to be the Voice?

JOAN. I am, of course. I turned to look. There was a great light filling the shadows behind me. The Voice was gentle and grave. I had never heard it before, and all it said to me was: "Be a good and sensible child, and go to church often". But I *was* good and I *did* go to church often—(*she rises*) and I promptly showed I was sensible by running away to safety. (*She sits on the stool down* C) I said nothing about it when I got home; but after supper I went back. The moon was rising; it shone on the white sheep; and that was all the light there was.

CAUCHON. Yes.

JOAN. And then came the second time. I could hear the bells ringing the noon-day Angelus. The light came again, brighter than the sun, and that time I saw him.

CAUCHON. You saw whom?

JOAN. A man in a white robe, with two white wings reaching from the ground to the sky. He didn't tell me his name that day, but later on I found out that he was the blessed St Michael. (*She rises and crosses slowly down* RC)

WARWICK (*to Cauchon*) Is it absolutely necessary to have her telling these absurdities all over again?

CAUCHON. Absolutely necessary, my lord.

(*The* PROMOTER *crosses and stands behind the left end of the fence* C. WARWICK *goes back to his corner in silence*)

JOAN (*in the deep voice of the Archangel*) Joan, go to the help of the King of France, and give him back his kingdom. (*She replies in her own voice*) Oh, sir, you haven't looked at me; I am only a young peasant girl, not a great captain who can lead an army. You will go and search out Robert de Beaudricourt, the Governor of Vaucouleurs. He will give you a suit of clothes to dress you like a man, and he will take you to the Dauphin. St Catherine and St Margaret will protect you. Please, please—(*she kneels*) pity me, holy sir. I'm a little girl, and I'm happy here alone in the fields. I've never had to be responsible for anything, except my sheep. If you will only look at me you will see I am small, and ignorant. The kingdom of France is far beyond anything I can do. But the King of France has famous captains, as strong as you could need, and they're used to doing these things. If they lose a battle they just cross all the dead men off their roll. But I should always remember I had killed them. Please have pity on me. (*She pauses*) No such thing. No pity. He had gone already—(*she rises*) and there I was, with France on my shoulders. Not to mention the work on the farm.

(FATHER *steps up stage*)

And my father who wasn't easy. (*She moves up* RC *to the fence, and sits on the floor in front of it*)

(*The sound of a church bell is heard off. The* PROMOTER *moves up* R *of the rostrum.*

The two SOLDIERS *exit up* R. MOTHER *moves to the stool down* R, *produces some knitting, sits and knits*)

FATHER (*moving to the fence down* R) Where has the girl got to?

MOTHER (*intent on her knitting*) She is out in the fields.

FATHER. Well, I was out in the fields, and I'm back home again. It's six o'clock. She's no business to be out in the fields.

BROTHER (*moving and lying on the floor* L *of Mother*) She's sitting under the Fairy Tree, staring at nothing. I saw her when I went to fetch in the bull.

(FATHER *turns up stage*)

PROMOTER. The Fairy Tree! Note that, gentlemen, if you will. Note the superstition. The beginning of witchcraft already. The Fairy Tree! I ask you to note that.

CAUCHON. There are Fairy Trees all over France, my lord Promoter. It's in our own interest not to refuse the fairies to these little girls.

PROMOTER (*primly*) We have our saints. That should be sufficient.

CAUCHON. It will be another matter when we come to the trial; I shan't spare her Voices then. But a little girl shall keep her fairies. (*Firmly*) And these discussions are under my charge.

(*The* PROMOTER *bows*)

FATHER (*moving behind the fence down* R; *bursting out afresh, to the Brother*) So that's where you say she is? And what does she think she's doing there, sitting under the tree?

BROTHER. Try and find out. She's just staring in front of her as if she was expecting something. And it isn't the first time, either.

(FATHER *leans over the fence as if to hit the* BROTHER, *who sits up and clutches Mother*)

FATHER. Well, why didn't you tell me when you saw her before, then? What do you think she was expecting, eh? Somebody, not something, idiot. She's got a lover, and you know it. (*He moves round* L *of the fence*) Give me my stick.

(BROTHER *rises, cowers, then gets the stick which is leaning against the wall* R)

MOTHER (*still knitting; gently*) You know quite well, Joan's as innocent as a baby.

FATHER (*moving to* L *of mother*) Maybe she is. And girls as innocent as babies can come to you one evening and hold up their faces to be kissed—(*he turns to* RC) and the next morning, though you've kept them locked in their room all night, what has happened? You can't see into their eyes at all. They're the devil, all at once. (*He turns up to the fence down* R *and faces up stage*)

PROMOTER (*with a step to* C; *raising a finger*) The word has been said, my lords, and by her father.

MOTHER. How do you know that? The day I married you I was as innocent as Joan, and I daresay you could look into my eyes just as well next morning.

FATHER (*turning; muttering*) That's nothing to do with it.

MOTHER. Who are these other girls you've known, then, that you've never told me about?

FATHER (*thundering to cover his embarrassment*) I tell you it's got nothing to do with it.

(*The sound of a church bell is heard off*)

(*To Mother*) We're not talking about other girls, we're talking about Joan. (*To Brother*) Hand me that stick. (*He moves to Brother and takes the stick from him*)

(Joan *rises*)

I'm going to look for her—(*he moves up* c) and if she's been meeting somebody on the quiet I'll skin them alive.

(Father *exits up* r.
Mother *and* Brother *exit down* r. *The* Promoter *crosses above the fence* c *to the right end of the fence up* r)

Joan (*smiling gently*) I was meeting someone on the quiet, and his solemn voice was saying: "Joan! Joan! What are you waiting for? There's a great sorrow in the realm of France." (*She takes a couple of steps down stage*) "Holy Sir of Heaven, I'm so afraid; I'm only a young village girl; surely you've made a mistake?" "Does God make mistakes, Joan?" (*She turns to her Judges*) How could I have answered "Yes"? (*She moves to the stool down* c *and sits*)

Promoter (*moving to* r *of Joan; shrugging*) You should have made the sign of the cross.

Joan. I did, and the Archangel made it, too, all the time keeping his eyes carefully on mine, and the church clock sounded.

Promoter. You should have cried: *Vade retro Satanus!*

Joan. I don't know Latin, my lord.

Promoter. Don't be an idiot! The devil understands French. You should have cried: Get thee behind me, foul Satan, and don't tempt me again.

Joan. But, my lord, it was St Michael.

Promoter (*sneering*) So he told you. And you were fool enough to believe him.

Joan. Yes, I believed him. He couldn't have been the devil. He shone with light; he was beautiful.

Promoter (*losing his temper*) So is the devil, so is the devil, I tell you.

Joan (*scandalized*) Oh, my lord.

Cauchon (*calming the Promoter with a gesture*) These subtle theological points, are proper for debating between ourselves, but they're beyond the understanding of this poor girl. No good is served by shocking her.

Joan (*to the Promoter*) You're telling a lie, Canon. I haven't any of your learning, but I know the devil is ugly, and all that's beautiful is the work of God.

Promoter (*sneering*) Very charming, simple and stupid. Do you think the devil is stupid? He's a thousand times more intelligent than you and I put together. (*He crosses above Joan to* l *of her*) Do you think when he comes to snare a soul he would come like a horror of the flesh, with black ploughed skin and a snouting tusk like a rhinoceros? If he did, souls would fly to virtue at the sight of him. I tell you he chooses a moonlit summer night, and comes with coaxing hands—(*he crosses below Joan and stands down* r) with eyes that receive you into them like water that drowns you, with naked woman's flesh, transparent, white—beautiful . . .

CAUCHON (*stopping him sternly*) Canon! You are losing your way. This is very far from Joan's devil, if she has seen one. I beg you not to confuse your devil with hers.

PROMOTER (*crossing above Joan to* R *of Cauchon; flushed and confused*) I beg your pardon, my lord; there is only one devil. (*He crosses to the fence down* R)

CAUCHON. Go on, Joan.

JOAN. Another time it was St Catherine and St Margaret who came to me. (*She turns to the Promoter with a slightly mischievous defiance*) They were beautiful, too.

PROMOTER (*moving* RC; *blushing, but unable to prevent himself*) Did they appear to you naked?

JOAN (*smiling*) Oh, my lord Promoter, do you imagine that God can't buy clothes for His saints?

(*The* PROMOTER, *confused, moves to the stool down* R *and sits.* CAUCHON *smiles.* WARWICK *laughs*)

CAUCHON. You see, you make us all smile with your questions, my lord Promoter. Be wise enough to keep your interruptions until we come to the serious heart of this business. And when we do so, particularly when we come to judge her, remember that the soul in this little arrogant body is in our care. Aren't you risking very much confusion in her mind, to suggest to her that the difference between good and evil is no more than a question of clothes? It is true, certainly, that our saints are traditionally represented as clothed; yet, on the other hand . . .

JOAN (*pointing to the Promoter*) Our Lord is naked on the cross.

CAUCHON (*turning to Joan*) I was going to say so, Joan, if you had not prevented me. It isn't for you to correct the reverend Canon. You forget who you are; you forget that we are your priests, your masters and your judges. Beware of your pride, Joan. If the devil one day wins you for his own, that is the way he will come to you.

JOAN. I know I am proud. But if God didn't mean me to be proud, why did He send an Archangel to see me, and saints with the light of heaven on them to speak to me? Why did He promise I should persuade all the people I have persuaded—men as learned and as wise as you—and say I should ride in white armour, with a bright sword given me by the King, to lead France into battle: and it has been so. He had only to leave me looking after the sheep, and I don't think pride would ever have entered my head.

CAUCHON. Weigh your words, Joan; weigh your thoughts. It is your Saviour you are accusing now.

JOAN (*crossing herself*) God guide me. His will be done, if His will is to make me proud and damned. That is His right, as well.

PROMOTER (*rising and moving* RC: *unable to contain himself*) Terrible! What she says is terrible! God's will to damn a soul? And you all listen to this without a murmur, my lords? I see here the seed of a fearful heresy which will one day tear the Church apart.

(*The* INQUISITOR *rises. He is an intelligent looking man, square and hard. He speaks with great quietness*)

INQUISITOR. Listen carefully to what I am going to ask you, Joan. Do you think you are in a state of grace at this moment?

(LADVENU *crosses to* R *of the fence up* R. *The* PROMOTER *and* WARWICK *step forward*)

JOAN (*firmly*) At what moment, my lord? Is it the beginning, when I hear my Voices, or the end, when I doubt and recant and the Church receives me again?

INQUISITOR. Don't evade my question. Do you think you are in a state of grace?

(*The* PRIESTS *watch Joan in silence; it seems a dangerous question*)

LADVENU (*crossing to* LC) My Lord Inquisitor, it is a formidable question for a simple girl who believes in all sincerity that God has called her. I ask that her reply shall not be held against her: she is quite unwittingly risking . . .

INQUISITOR. Quiet, Brother Ladvenu. I ask what I consider good to ask. Let her answer my question. Do you think you are in a state of grace, Joan?

(LADVENU *moves to* L *of Joan*)

JOAN (*rising and turning to the Inquisitor*) If I am not, may God in His goodness set me there. If I am, may God in His goodness keep me so.

LADVENU (*quietly*) Well answered, Joan. (*He moves a step or two up* C)

(JOAN *crosses to the stool down* R *and sits*)

PROMOTER (*annoyed by Joan's success; muttering to Ladvenu*) What of it? The devil has cunning, or he wouldn't be the devil. It isn't the first time he has been asked that question. We know what he is; he has his answers all ready.

(*The* PROMOTER *exits* RC. LADVENU *moves below the fence down* R.
The INQUISITOR *exits over the rostrum*)

WARWICK (*crossing to* R *of Cauchon; bored*) No doubt this is all very interesting, my lord, but if you go on at this rate we shall never get to the trial, never have her burnt, never get anywhere. I said she could take us over the old ground again, if you thought it so necessary, but let her get on with it. And let us come to the essentials. His Majesty's Government have to discredit this wretched little Charles Valois, at once; it's imperative that we should let Christendom know—(*he crosses to* C) that the Coronation was all a humbug, the performance of a witch, a heretic, an army's whore.

(LADVENU *turns to Warwick*)

CAUCHON. My lord, we're trying her only for heresy.

WARWICK. I know that; but I have to make more of it for the sake of the troops. The findings of your trial, I'm afraid, will be too rarefied for my soldiers. (*He moves above the stool down* C) Propaganda, my lord Bishop, is black or white. The main thing is to say something pretty staggering, and repeat it often enough until you turn it into a truth. It's a new idea, but, believe me, it will make its way. The essential thing, so far as I am concerned, is that the girl should be a nonentity, whatever she is in fact. And what she is in fact is of no particular importance to His Majesty's Government. Personally, I must admit, I find the girl attractive. The way she takes the wind out of your sails gives me a lot of pleasure; and her seat on a horse is very good—(*he picks up the stool*) that's rare in a woman. If the circumstances had been different, and she had belonged to my own set—(*he moves up* R *of the rostrum, puts the stool on the second step and leans on it*) I should have enjoyed a day's hunting with her. But unfortunately there's been this damned Coronation, and that was nobody's notion but hers. Really, my lord, what impudence! To dare to pick France out of our pockets, and pilfer the English heritage. Luckily, God is on the side of England, as he satisfactorily proved at Agincourt. God and our right. Two ideas completely synonymous. And moreover, inscribed on our coat-of-arms. (*He picks up the stool*) So rattle her through the rest of it, and have her burned, and not so much talk. Earlier on I was joking. I give it ten years, and this whole incident will have been forgotten.

(LADVENU *crosses down* R.

A SOLDIER *enters* LC. *He places the fence* C *up and downstage* C. *A second* SOLDIER *enters* RC. *He places the fence up* RC *up and downstage* RC. *A third* SOLDIER *enters down* R. *He places the fence down* R *on and off stage, starting from the downstage end of the fence* RC, *in its new position. The formation is a bridge. See Ground Plan B. The* SOLDIERS *exit*)

CAUCHON (*sighing*) God grant so, my lord. (*He rises*)

(FATHER *enters up* R. *He carries his stick*)

WARWICK (*with a step to* C) Where had we got to?

FATHER (*moving down* RC) To where I was going out to find her, sitting under her tree, waiting to get herself into trouble, the little bitch. And I can tell you she'll be sorry she ever began it. (*He moves to Joan and bangs her stool with his stick*)

(Joan *is startled*)

What are you doing here, eh? Tell me what you're waiting about here for, when you know you ought to be indoors, eating your supper.

(Warwick, *taking the stool with him, exits with* Cauchon LC. Ladvenu *exits down* R)

Joan (*shy at being surprised; stammering*) I didn't know it was so late. I had lost count of the time. (*She rises and crosses to* C *of the bridge*)

Father (*following to* R *of Joan*) That's it, you lost count of the time. And what else have you lost that you daren't tell me? (*He shakes her abominably*) Who made you forget it was so late? I heard you as I came along, calling out good-bye to somebody. Well, who was it?

Joan. St Michael, Father.

(Father *goes to hit* Joan *with his stick. She stumbles down* C *and falls to the ground*)

Father. You make fun at your father, you'll be sorry. (*He moves to* R *of Joan*) I won't have any girl of mine sitting out in the fields waiting for any man who wants to find her. You'll marry the decent fellow we choose for you, or I'll break every bone in your body.

Joan. I've done nothing wrong, Father—(*she kneels up*) truthfully it was the blessed St Michael who spoke to me and St Margaret and St Catherine . . .

Father. Why should St Michael speak to you, you little idiot? Does he speak to me? Natural enough, if he had something to say to us, he'd say it to me, the head of the family. Does he speak to our priest? (*He shakes her*)

Joan. Father, stop shaking me and try to understand. I'm so alone, and they want me to do so much. For three years I've been trying not to believe them. I can't go on fighting them all by myself. I've got to do what they say.

Father (*moving to the right fence of the bridge and leaning on it*) The Voices you hear? Do you want to drive me mad?

Joan. They say it can't wait any longer; the time has come when I have to say yes. (*She rises and faces him*)

Father. What can't wait any longer, idiot? What are they telling you to do, what you call these Voices?

Joan. They tell me to go and save the realm of France which is in grave danger of being destroyed. That's true, isn't it?

Father (*turning to her*) Heavens above! Of course the realm of France is in danger of being destroyed. It isn't the first time, and it won't be the last; and she always gets out of it. Leave it in God's hands; there's nothing you can do about it, you poor girl. Even a man can't do anything about it, unless he's a soldier. (*He turns back to the bridge*)

JOAN. But I can. My Voices have said so.

FATHER (*moving down* R *and making a large circle around Joan to the rostrum* L; *laughing*) Oh, you can, can you? Dear me! You're sharper than all our great captains, of course, who can't do anything these days except be beaten every time they fight?

JOAN (*facing front*) Yes, Father.

FATHER (*sitting* C *of the bottom step of the rostrum*) "Yes, Father." Perhaps you're not a bad girl, but worse. You're a mad, idiot girl. What do you think you can do, then, poor idiot?

JOAN. What my Voices tell me. I can ask the Squire of Beaudricourt for an armed escort. And when I've got my escort, I can go straight to the Dauphin at Chinon, to tell him that he's the rightful King; and I can lead him out at the head of the army, and then we can drive the English out of France.

FATHER (*suddenly understanding; removing his belt*) Now you're explaining yourself, at last, you filthy little slut. You want to go off with the soldiers, like the lowest of the low?

JOAN (*smiling mysteriously*) No, Father, like the highest under God, riding first into the battle, and not looking back until I have saved France. (*Suddenly sad*) And after that is done, what happens is God's will.

FATHER. I've heard enough shameless lying. (*He rises, puts his stick on the rostrum, moves to Joan and throws her on to the rostrum*) I'll teach you what happens to girls who go chasing after soldiers, pretending to save France. (*He savagely and unmercifully beats her with his belt*)

JOAN (*crying*) Stop, Father, stop, stop!

(LADVENU, WARWICK *and* CAUCHON, *after three blows, enter* RC *and stand* R *of the bridge rail. As they speak,* FATHER *mimes the beating in silence*)

LADVENU (*very pale*) This must be stopped! He means to injure her.

CAUCHON (*gently*) We can do nothing, Brother Ladvenu. At this part of the story we have never met Joan; we don't get to know her until the trial. We can only act our parts, each his own, good or bad, as they are written, and in his turn.

(FATHER *stops the beating, throws Joan down* C *and puts on his belt*)

And later on, you know, we shall do worse things than this to her. (*He turns to Warwick*) This domestic scene is not very pleasant to witness, my lord?

WARWICK (*with a gesture*) Why not? We're firm believers in

corporal punishment in England; it forms the character. I myself have been flogged many times as a boy; and I took it extremely well.

(FATHER *wipes the sweat off his forehead, and shouts at* JOAN, *lying crumpled at his feet*)

FATHER. There! You carrion! Do you still want to save France? (*He turns to the others, rather ashamed of himself*) Well, sirs, what would you have done in my place if your daughter had said that to you?

(WARWICK, CAUCHON and LADVENU *exit* RC.
MOTHER *enters up* R)

MOTHER (*moving to* R *of Father*) Have you killed her?
FATHER. Not this time. But if she talks any more about going off with the soldiers, I'll drown that girl of yours in the river with my own hands; do you hear me? (*He moves to the rostrum and picks up his stick*) And if I'm nowhere about, I give her brothers full permission to do it for me.

(FATHER *strides off* LC)

MOTHER (*kneeling* R *of Joan*) Joan, my little Joan, my little Joan. Did he hurt you?

(JOAN *sits up and gives a pathetic smile when she recognizes her mother*)

JOAN. Yes. He meant me to feel it.
MOTHER. Now, now, now, you don't have to upset yourself. You remember when you were little we used to rock away your nightmares together. But now you're nearly a woman: nearly too big to hold in my arms any more. I can tell you it's no good breaking your heart to make men understand anything. Who is it, then, Joanie? You can tell your mother. Don't you even know his name, perhaps? And yet I don't know but it must be someone in the village. Why, your father might even agree to him; he's not against a good marriage for you. We might even be able to persuade him he chose the boy himself, the poor old stupid.
JOAN. It isn't marriage that I have to think of, Mother. The blessed St Michael has told me I should leave the village, put on a man's clothes, and go and find his highness the Dauphin, to save the realm of France.
MOTHER (*rising; severely*) Joan, I speak nicely and gently to you, but I won't have you talking wickedness. And I won't have you put on a man's clothes, not if you beg at my grave.
JOAN. But, Mother, I should have to, if I'm to ride horseback. It's the blessed St Michael who says so.
MOTHER. I don't care what the blessed St Michael says, you shall never go off on a horse. Joan of Arc on a horse!

JOAN (*rising*) But if I don't ride a horse, how can I lead the soldiers?

MOTHER. And you won't go with the soldiers, either, you wicked girl. I'd rather see you cold and dead. You see, now you make me talk the same as your father. There are some things we feel the same about. A daughter spins, and scrubs, and stays at home. Your grandmother never left this village, and neither have I—(*she moves to the centre of the bridge and turns to Joan*) and neither will you, and when you have a daughter of your own, neither will she. (*She suddenly bursts into tears*) Going off with the soldiers! Do you want to kill me?

(*The sound of a church bell is heard off.* JOAN *throws herself at her Mother's feet, with her arms around her waist, and weeps*)

JOAN. No, Mother.

MOTHER. You do, I see you do. You'll destroy yourself in the end if you don't soon get these thoughts out of your head.

(MOTHER *exits up* R)

JOAN (*facing front*) You see, blessed St Michael, it isn't possible; they won't ever understand. No-one will. (*She kneels up*) It is better that I should give up at once. Our Lord has said that we have to obey our father and mother. (*She speaks with the voice of the Archangel*) " But first, Joan, you have to obey God." But if God commands the impossible? "Then you have to attempt the impossible, calmly and quietly. It is a cause for pride, Joan, that God gives you something of His burden to carry. He doesn't ask the impossible of everybody, but He does ask it of you. That is all." (*She looks up. Simply*) Well, I will go. (*She rises*) It's all decided.

(*The "Horse" music is heard and continues until the "Fight" music*)

I shall go and find my Uncle Durand. With him I always get my own way. (*She runs up to the top of the rostrum* L) He's as easy to manage as a tame sparrow. I shall kiss him on both cheeks, and on the top of his head, and sit on his lap, and he will say: "Oh, Lord, oh, Lord", and take me to Vaucouleurs. (*She turns to exit* L)

(BROTHER *runs on up* R)

BROTHER (*crossing to the foot of the rostrum*) You're a silly donkey! Why did you have to go and tell the old people all that stuff? Next time, if you give me a ha'penny, I won't say a word about where I saw you.

(*The "Fight" music is heard and continues until* JOAN *and* BROTHER *exit*)

JOAN. Oh, so it was you who told them—(*she leaps on to Brother, clasps her legs round his waist and beats his chest*) you beastly little sneak. Take that for your ha'penny lardy head.

(BROTHER *drops Joan as he swings round to* L *of her. He runs to* L *of the fence* LC. *Joan goes to* R *of the fence* LC. *They pick it up between them and struggle round with it until it is running on and off from the post* C *to* L, *where they set it down*)

So it was you who told them with your mouth always open.

BROTHER. And I'll tell them again if you don't keep away. (*He runs to the fence up and down* RC, *jumps over it, then goes to the fence down* R, *picks it up and places it with one end against the upstage side of the arch, and the other end against the corner of the downstage flat*)

(JOAN *picks up the fence* RC *and places it with one end against the post* C, *and the other against the upstage side of the arch*)

Tell tales out of school—duck him in a muddy pool. (*He runs through the arch and round the back of the fence to* C)

(JOAN *meets Brother* C *and catches him*)

JOAN. I'll teach you to tell tales about me. (*She hits him*)

BROTHER. Tell-tale-tit your tongue shall be split.

(JOAN *pulls his hair and thrashes him.*
BROTHER *yells and runs off down* L.
JOAN *runs off after Brother.*
The moment the chase starts, a* SOLDIER *enters down* R *with two trestles, which he places* RC. *Two* SOLDIERS *enter down* L, *take the top and the middle rostrum from* LC *and cross to* RC. *They place the middle rostrum on top of the trestles, making a table of it. They place the top rostrum alongside the right side of the table, forming a seat. One* SOLDIER *moves the stool down* R *and places it below the table. The* SOLDIER, *having placed the trestles, exits, and re-enters with a tray on which there is a bowl of fruit, a plate, a tankard and a jug of wine. He places them in the centre of the table. See Ground Plan C.*
The* SOLDIERS *exit.*
ROBERT DE BEAUDRICOURT, SQUIRE OF VAUCOULEURS, enters* LC *and crosses to* L *of the table* RC)

BEAUDRICOURT. Well, what is it? What does she want? What is it she wants, the infernal nuisance? (*He turns*) What's this nonsensical story I hear . . .?

(JOAN *runs in* LC *and collides head first with Beaudricourt's great paunch.* BEAUDRICOURT *is half-winded, gives a yell of pain, grabs Joan by her arms, and, apoplectic with rage, lifts her level with his nose*)

What the devil do you want, you horrible mosquito? What the devil do you mean, playing the fool outside my gates for three

days on end? What the devil are these tales you've been telling
the guards until their eyes pop out as far as their noses? (*He puts
her down*)

JOAN. I want a horse, my lord, a man's clothes, and an escort,
to go to Chinon to see his highness the Dauphin.

BEAUDRICOURT. And my boot, you want that, too, of course?

JOAN. If you like, my lord, and a good clout, as long as I get
the horse as well.

BEAUDRICOURT. You know about me and you know what I
want; the village girls have told you all about it, haven't they?
They come along to see me, usually to beg for the life of a brother,
or their old father who's been caught poaching on my lands.
(*He crosses slowly behind Joan to L of her*) If the girl is pretty, I
always hook him down off the gallows, being amiable at heart.
If she's ugly, I hang the old chap, to make an example of him.
But it's always the pretty ones who come; they manage to dig
up one in the family somehow; with the admirable result that I
have a fine reputation for benevolence in the neighbourhood. So
now you know the rate of exchange, and we can come to terms.
(*He crosses below Joan to the bench down R, and sits on the downstage
end, facing her*)

JOAN (*simply*) I don't know what you're trying to say, my
lord. The blessed St Michael sent me to you.

BEAUDRICOURT (*anxiously crossing himself*) You don't have to
bring the saints into this. That was all right for the guards, to
get you in to see me. But now you're here, and you can leave the
saints in their proper places. (*He pours wine for himself*) And I
wouldn't be surprised if you get your horse. An old jade for a
young maid; it's a reasonable bargain. Are you a virgin?

JOAN. Yes, my lord.

BEAUDRICOURT (*looking at her all the time*) I agree to the horse.

JOAN. That isn't all I want, my lord.

BEAUDRICOURT. A greedy child, I see. Well, go on; you're
amusing me. If I pay well for my pleasures it helps me to believe
I really want them. You understand where this conversation is
leading?

JOAN (*frankly*) No, my lord.

BEAUDRICOURT. Splendid. The bed's no place for brains. What
else do you want beside the horse? The taxes are coming in very
well this autumn; I don't mind being generous. (*He takes a knife
from his belt and peels an apple*)

JOAN (*moving to L of the table*) An escort of men-at-arms, my
lord, to accompany me to Chinon.

BEAUDRICOURT (*changing his tone*) Now, listen to me: if we're to
get on together—I may be easy-going, but I won't stand any
impudence. Why do you want to go to Chinon?

JOAN. To find his highness the Dauphin.

BEAUDRICOURT. Well, well, you mean to get on. Why not the

Duke of Burgundy while you're about it? In theory, you might have a sporting chance with him: the Duke's as hot as a buck rabbit. Whereas, as you probably know, the Dauphin when it comes to war and women . . . I don't know what you expect to get from him.

JOAN. An army, my lord, which I can lead to rescue Orleans.

(BEAUDRICOURT, *startled, drops his knife on to the plate, rises and moves about the table to* C)

BEAUDRICOURT. Ah! If you're mad it's another thing altogether. I'm not getting involved in any scandal. (*He calls*) Hey, there, Boudousse!

(BOUDOUSSE, *a guard, enters* LC)

Take her away and give her a ducking.

(*The* GUARD *moves to Joan and grabs her arms*)

And then lock her up. You can send her back to her father tomorrow evening.

(*The* GUARD *leads* JOAN *behind the fence up* LC)

But no beating, I don't want any trouble; the girl's mad. (*He moves below the fence* LC)

JOAN (*leaning over the fence; calmly*) You can lock me up, my lord: I don't mind that; but when they let me out tomorrow evening I shall come back again. So it would be simpler if you let me talk to you now.

BEAUDRICOURT (*thumping the rostrum*) Ten million thunders! (*To the Guard*) Get back to your post. (*To Joan*) Don't I frighten you?

(*The* GUARD *releases* JOAN, *moves* L *and stops*)

JOAN. No, my lord. Not at all.

(*The* GUARD *sniggers*)

BEAUDRICOURT (*to the Guard*) You don't need to stand about listening to this.

(*The* GUARD *exits* LC)

(*When the Guard has gone. Uneasily*) And why don't I frighten you? I frighten everybody.

JOAN (*quietly*) Because you are very good, my lord.

BEAUDRICOURT. Good? Good? I've told you, that depends on the price. (*He crosses to* L *of the table*)

JOAN. And what's more, very intelligent.

(BEAUDRICOURT *turns to* JOAN)

There are many people I will have to convince before I can do everything my Voices want; so it's lucky—(*she crosses to* L *of him*) the first person I have to deal with, the one everything really depends on, should turn out to be the most intelligent.

(BEAUDRICOURT, *slightly puzzled, pours himself some wine*)

BEAUDRICOURT (*in a casual voice*) You're an odd girl, in your way. How did you come to notice that I'm intelligent?

JOAN. Because you're very handsome, my lord.

BEAUDRICOURT (*with a furtive glance at his reflection in the metal jug*) Oh, tush! I suppose, twenty years ago, I might say that I pleased the ladies; and I've taken care of myself, not let myself get too old too soon; that's all it is. It's quite peculiar and unsettling to have a conversation like this with a farm girl I've never heard of, who happens to drop in like a stray kitten. (*He sighs, and with the tankard in his hand, crosses below Joan to* C) On the whole I vegetate here. My lieutenants are a poor bunch: hardly a brain between them. And while we're on the subject, what's this connexion you find between intellect and beauty? (*He moves down* C) I've usually heard quite the opposite: handsome people are always stupid; that's the general opinion.

JOAN. That's the opinion of the plain people—(*she sits on the stool below the table*) who like to believe God can't manage both things at once.

BEAUDRICOURT (*flattered*) Ah well, you've made a point there. But then, take myself, for example. (*With a step towards her*) I know, as you so kindly say, I'm not one of the plain people; but I wonder sometimes, am I, after all, very intelligent? No, no don't protest. (*He moves a little up* C) It's a question I have to ask now and again. I can tell you this, between ourselves, as you're not anyone in particular. Obviously I'm more intelligent than my lieutenants, that's only natural, being officer in command. If that wasn't an established fact there wouldn't be an army at all. (*He moves slowly to* R *of the rostrum* LC) But even so, I sometimes meet with problems which I find very troublesome. They ask me to decide something, some tactical or administrative point, and quite suddenly, I don't know why, my mind is a blank. There it is, nothing but a sort of fog. Mark you, nobody knows that. I get out of it, without my face showing any change of expression; I make a decision all right. (*He steps on to the rostrum* LC) And that's the essential thing when you're in command, of course: make a decision, whatever it is. Until you've had some experience you're apt to get flustered: but you realize after a bit—(*he sits on the upper rostrum*) it all amounts to the same thing, whatever you decide. Still, I should like to see myself doing better. Vaucouleurs, as you see, is of no great size. I'm looking forward to the day when I make a really important decision: one of those momentous decisions, of great consequence to the nation: not a question of somebody who hasn't paid his taxes, or half a dozen prisoners to be hanged—(*he rises*) but something a bit exceptional, which would get me noticed and talked about higher up. (*He stops dreaming, rises and looks at Joan*) I don't know what in the world I'm doing, telling you all this. You can't do anything about it, and God help you, you're half crazy into the bargain. (*He crosses to* L *of Joan*)

JOAN (*smiling gently*) I know why. (*She rises*) I knew it would happen, because my Voices told me so.

(BEAUDRICOURT *turns away* L)

Listen, Robert . . . (*She sits on the downstage edge of the table, with her feet on the stool*)

BEAUDRICOURT (*turning to her; startled*) What are you doing, calling me by my Christian name?

JOAN. It's God's name for you, Robert . . .

(BEAUDRICOURT *starts to interrupt*)

Now listen, Robert——

(BEAUDRICOURT *crosses below Joan to* R *of her*)

—and don't bluster again, because it isn't any use. What is the important decision, which will get you noticed and talked about higher up? I can tell you, Robert. It's me.

BEAUDRICOURT. What are you talking about? (*He puts his arm around Joan's shoulder*)

JOAN. I'll tell you, if you'll listen. (*She removes his arm*) First of all, you have to stop thinking of me as a woman. It's getting you confused. I don't interest you much, anyway, do I?

(BEAUDRICOURT, *afraid of being cheated, hesitates*)

(*She flares up and grabs the tankard from him*) Robert, if you want to help yourself, you have to help me, too. When I tell you the truth, acknowledge it and say "Yes": otherwise we shall never get anywhere.

BEAUDRICOURT (*sitting on the downstage end of the bench; muttering, rather shame-faced*) Well, no . . .

JOAN (*severely*) What do you mean, "no"?

BEAUDRICOURT. I mean, yes, it's true. You don't interest me. (*Politely*) Though, mind you, you're a pretty enough little thing . . .

JOAN. All right, you don't have to think you've upset me. I'm very happy the point is cleared up. And now you can imagine you have already given me the suit of clothes I asked for, and we can discuss things together, sensibly and calmly, as man to man.

BEAUDRICOURT (*still suspicious*) Discuss what?

JOAN. Your decision, Robert. Your great achievement which will make everyone take notice of you. Think of all of them, there at Bourges. They don't know whether they're praying or cursing, or which saint to turn to next. The English are everywhere, and you know the French army. Good boys, who have still got fight in them, but they're discouraged. They've got it into their heads that the English will always be the strongest, and there's nothing to be done. Of course there's La Hire, and there's Xantrailles: prize angry bulls: they always want to charge in head first. They belong among the champions of single combat, who don't understand how to use their cannons. They're wonderful at getting killed—(*she rises and moves down* c) but it isn't any help. That's true, isn't it, Robert? You can't treat war like a tournament. You have to win. You have to be cunning. (*She touches her forehead*) You have to wage it here. With all your intelligence, Robert, you know that better than I do. (*She moves a little up* c)

BEAUDRICOURT (*rising*) I've always said so. Nowadays we don't think enough. Take my lieutenants—(*he moves slowly* RC) always spoiling for a fight, and that's all they can think of. And the men who know how to think get overlooked: nobody dreams of using them.

JOAN (*crossing above him to the table*) Nobody. So they have to think for themselves. (*She pours some wine into the tankard*) It's a lucky thing you have had such a tremendous idea. It's bound to alter everything. (*She gives him the tankard, then moves above the table to* R *of it*)

BEAUDRICOURT (*uneasily*) I have an idea? (*He moves slowly below the table*)

JOAN. Don't question it, Robert; be very proud of it. Your brain is working at great speed, clearly, concisely. It's a sad thing to think that, in the whole of France at this moment, no-one sees things clearly, except you.

BEAUDRICOURT. You believe so?

JOAN (*moving to* R *of him*) I tell you so.

BEAUDRICOURT. And what is it I see? (*He sits on the stool below the table*)

JOAN (*kneeling* R *of him*) You see simply that the people of France have to be given a spirit and a faith. And this is where you show yourself to be so remarkable. You say to yourself: Here's a little peasant girl, of no consequence at all; all right. If by any chance she really has been sent by God, then nothing could stop her, and it can't be proved one way or the other whether God sent her or not. She certainly got in to see me, without my permission, and I've been listening to her for half an hour; nobody could deny that. And then, like a sword of lightning, the idea strikes home to you. You say to yourself: If she has the power to convince me, why shouldn't she convince the Dauphin and Dunois and the Archbishop? They're men, just as I'm a man; as a matter of fact, between ourselves, rather less intelligent. Moreover, why shouldn't she convince our soldiers that the English in the main are exactly like themselves, half courage and half a wish to save their skins; pummel them hard enough at the right moment, and you send them staggering out of Orleans. (*She rises*) It's magnificent how you marshal the whole situation in your mind. What our fellows need, you are saying to yourself: what they need is someone to rouse their spirit, and prove to them that God is still with them. This is where you show yourself a born leader.

BEAUDRICOURT (*pitifully*) You think that?

JOAN (*crossing below Beaudricourt to L of him*) I know it. And soon so will everyone else. (*She turns to him*) Like all great politicians, you're a realist, Robert. You say to yourself: I, Beaudricourt, have my doubts about her coming from God, but I'll send her off to them, and if they think she is, it will have the same effect whether it's true or false. (*She turns to c*) By a stroke of good luck my courier is leaving for Bourges tomorrow morning . . .

BEAUDRICOURT (*rising*) Who told you that? It's a secret.

JOAN (*turning to him*) I found it out. I pick half a dozen strong men for an escort, give her a horse and send her off with the courier. At Chinon, as far as I can see, she will work things out for herself. (*She looks admiringly at him*) My word, my word, Robert!

BEAUDRICOURT. What?

JOAN. You have a marvellous intelligence to think of all that.

BEAUDRICOURT (*wiping his forehead; worn out*) Yes. (*He sits on the stool below the table*)

JOAN (*moving to L of him*) Only, please give me a quiet horse, because I don't know how to ride one yet.

BEAUDRICOURT (*delighted*) You're going to break your neck, my girl.

(JOAN *takes the tankard from Beaudricourt, moves to L of the table, and refills it*)

JOAN. I don't think so. St Michael will hold me on. I tell you what, Robert: I'll have a wager with you.

(BEAUDRICOURT *rises and moves to L of Joan*)

(*She hands him the tankard*) I'll bet you a suit of clothes—the man's clothes which you still haven't said you'll give me—against a punch on the nose.

(BEAUDRICOURT *drinks*)

Bring two horses into the courtyard and we'll gallop them together. If I fall off, you can lose faith in me. (*She takes the tankard from him, drinks from it, then puts it on the tray*) Is that fair? (*She offers him her hand*) Agreed? And whoever doesn't pay up is a man of mud.

BEAUDRICOURT (*shaking hands with her*) Agreed. I need to move about a bit. I wouldn't have believed how tiring it is to think so much. (*He moves a little up* C *and calls*) Boudousse!

(*The* GUARD *enters* LC *and stands behind the fence* LC)

GUARD. Do I take her away and give her a ducking, sir?
BEAUDRICOURT. No, you idiot! You fetch her some breeches, and bring us a couple of horses. We're taking a gallop together.
GUARD. But what about the Council, sir?

(*"Horse" music is heard*)

It's four o'clock.
BEAUDRICOURT. It can wait till tomorrow. Today I've used my brains quite enough.

(BEAUDRICOURT *crosses above the fence* LC *and exits* LC.
JOAN *follows him off. As she passes the astonished* GUARD, *she sticks out her tongue. The* GUARD *turns up stage. During the beginning of the following scene, the stage is re-set as follows.*
Three SOLDIERS *enter down* R. *The* 1ST SOLDIER *takes the tray from the table, exits with it down* R, *then re-enters. The* 2ND SOLDIER *goes below the table, picks up the stool and puts it on the table. The* 3RD SOLDIER *goes to the top end of the table. The* 2ND *and* 3RD SOLDIERS *pick up the bench and place it on the table. They then lift the table with the bench on it. The* 1ST SOLDIER *picks up the trestles and exits with them down* R. *The* 2ND *and* 3RD SOLDIERS *then turn on and off stage* RC *and put the "table-top" on the floor. They then take the "bench" from the "table" and place it in front of the top. They place the stool on the rostrum so formed. It now forms a small throne. During this the* GUARD *moves* RC *and places the fence up and down* RC, *across stage until it is behind and almost parallel to the throne. He places the fence up* RC *behind the arch* R. *See Ground Plan D.*
The SOLDIERS *and the* GUARD *exit.*
WARWICK *and* CAUCHON *enter up* R *and cross behind the fence* LC)

WARWICK. I can see this girl had quality. Very entertaining, to watch her playing the old fish; didn't you think so?
CAUCHON. Rather too crude for my taste, my lord. Something subtler than that will be needed when she comes to deal with Charles. (*He moves down* C)
WARWICK (*crossing to* R *of Cauchon*) My lord Bishop, the tricks that you and I use in our way of business aren't so remarkably different from hers. Whether we're ruling the world with a mace or a crozier, in the long run, we do it by persuading fools that what we make them think is their own opinion. No need for any intervention of God in that. Which is why I found it so entertaining. (*He bows politely towards Cauchon*) Entertaining, at least, if one isn't professionally concerned, of course, as you are. Have

you faith yourself, my lord Bishop? Forgive my bluntness; but between ourselves, I'm interested to know.

CAUCHON (*simply*) A child's faith, my lord. And that is why I shall make problems for you during the trial, and why we shall go as far as ever we can to save Joan, even though we have been sincere collaborators with the English rule, which seemed to us then the only reasonable solution to chaos. It was very easy for those who were at Bourges to call us traitors, when they had the protection of the French army. We were in occupied Rouen.

WARWICK. I don't like the word "occupied". You were quite simply on His Majesty's territory.

CAUCHON. In the midst of His Majesty's army, and the execution of His Majesty's hostages; submitting to the curfew, and the condescension of His Majesty's food-supplies. We were men, with the frailty of men, who wanted to go on living, and yet at the same time to save Joan if we could. It was not, in any way, a happy part that we were called on to play.

WARWICK (*smiling*) There was nothing to stop you becoming martyrs, my dear fellow, if that would have made it more inspiring for you. My eight hundred soldiers were quite ready.

CAUCHON. We knew it. They took great pleasure in shouting their insults at us, hammering on the door with the butts of their halberds, to remind us they were there. We temporized for nine months before we would deliver Joan up to you; this little girl, forsaken by everyone; nine months to make her say "yes". Future times will be pleased to say we were barbarous. But I fancy, for all their fine principles, they will take to expediency faster than we did; in every camp.

WARWICK (*moving below the rostrum* R) Nine months, that's quite true. What a difficult confinement this trial has been. Our Holy Mother Church takes her time, when she's asked to give birth to a small matter of policy. But the nightmare is over. The mother and child are both doing well. (*He sits* C *of the rostrum* R)

CAUCHON (*moving to* L *of the rostrum* R) I have pondered deeply over these things, my lord. The health of the mother, as you put it, is our one concern. And that is why, when we saw there could be no alternative, we sacrificed the child in good faith. Ever since that day of Joan's arrest, God has been dead to us. Neither she, whatever she may imagine, nor we, certainly, have heard Him any more. We have gone on, following our daily custom; our pre-eminent duty, to defend the old house, this great and wise human building which is all that remains to us in the absence of God. From the time we were fifteen years old, we were taught how to defend it. Joan had no such help, and yet, though her faith fell on dreadful days, when she was left alone by men and by God, she also has gone on, recovering at once after the single moment when she weakened, bearing herself with her curious mixture of humility and insolence, or grandeur and good sense, even up to execution and death. We weren't able to understand it then; we had our eyes buried in our mother's skirts, like children grown old. And yet, precisely in this loneliness, in the desert of a vanished God, in the privation and misery of the animal, the man is indeed great who continues to lift his head. Greatly alone.

WARWICK. Yes, well, no doubt. But if our business is politics we can't afford to brood about such men. We seem fated, as a rule, to meet them among the people we condemn to execution.

CAUCHON (*after a pause; quietly*) It is a consolation to me sometimes to think of those old priests who, though they were deeply offended by her insolent answers, nevertheless, even with English swords at their back—(*he crosses down* R) tried for nine months not to commit the irreparable.

WARWICK (*rising*) Nothing is irreparable in politics. I tell you we shall raise a handsome statue to her in London one day, when the right time comes.

> (*"Cuckoo" music is heard.*
> A SOLDIER *enters* LC *and opens up the fence* LC. *Two* SOLDIERS *follow him on, carrying the throne chair which they place on the rostrum* LC. *See Ground Plan D.*
> *The* SOLDIERS *exit.*)

But now let's come to Chinon, my lord.

> (CHARLES, THE DAUPHIN, *enters up* R *and crosses to the throne* LC. *He is reading and carrying a cup-and-ball. He crosses while* WARWICK *is speaking*)

I've got a profound disrespect for that lounging little idler, Charles—(*he moves up* RC) but he's a character who never fails to amuse me.

> (WARWICK *and* CAUCHON *exit* RC
> AGNES SOREL *enters up* R, *crosses and stands above the rostrum* LC. CHARLES *sits on the throne.*
> THE YOUNG QUEEN *and* QUEEN YOLANDE *follow Agnes in up* R. *The* QUEEN *stands up* C. YOLANDE *crosses and sits on the stool on the rostrum* RC. *The ladies all carry embroidery frames*)

AGNES. Charles, it's impossible! You can't let me appear at the ball looking such a frump. Your mistress in one of last year's steeple-hats. (*She moves to the downstage corner of the rostrum* LC *and sits on it*)

QUEEN (*moving to Charles*) And your Queen, Charles. The Queen of France. What would they say? (*She sits on the upstage corner of the rostrum* LC)

CHARLES (*playing cup-and-ball*) They would say the King of France isn't worth a farthing. Which is quite right.

AGNES. Imagine, Charles, if they're wearing our newest fashions over there before we are.

CHARLES. At least they pay for them. Fashion is practically the only thing we can sell them: our fashions and our cooking. They are the only things which still give us some prestige with the foreigners.

YOLANDE. We have to defend this prestige, Charles. A steeple-hat the English have never seen before might be as good as a great victory.

CHARLES (*with a dry laugh*) A victory which isn't going to stop them making off with Orleans, Mother-in-law. How much did you say these steeple-hats would come to?

AGNES. Six thousand francs, my darling.

(CHARLES *reacts*)

That's next to nothing, when you remember they're completely embroidered with pearls.

CHARLES. Six thousand francs! But where do you think I can find six thousand francs, you poor little fool?

QUEEN (*softly*) Twelve thousand francs, Charles, because there are two of us, remember. (*She rises*) You wouldn't want your mistress to be better dressed than your wife. (*She kneels on the rostrum*)

CHARLES. Twelve thousand francs! They've gone out of their minds.

AGNES (*rising and kneeling on the rostrum*) Of course there's a simpler model, but I wouldn't advise it. You would forfeit the moral effect we should have on the stupid English. And that, after all, is the effect we're after.

CHARLES. Twelve thousand francs.

AGNES }
QUEEN } (*together*) Yes.

CHARLES. Enough to pay three-quarters of Dunois's army. I don't understand how you can encourage them, Mother-in-law, a woman of your good judgement. (*He stands up on his throne*)

YOLANDE. It's because I'm a woman of good judgement that I support them, Charles. Have you ever found me opposing anything that might be for your good or the dignity of the throne? I am the mother of your Queen, and yet it was I who introduced you to Agnes when I saw clearly how it might help you.

(CHARLES *sits on his throne with his feet up and reads*)

QUEEN (*crossing to Yolande*) Please, Mother, don't brag about it.

(*She sits on the downstage corner of the rostrum* RC)

YOLANDE. Daughter, Agnes is a very charming girl who perfectly knows her place. Besides, you will thank me later on: one sleeps so much better alone. And Charles is far more manly since he knew Agnes. You are more manly, aren't you, Charles?

CHARLES. Yes. Yesterday I said "No" to the Archbishop. He

tried to scare me, he sent La Tremouille in first to roar at me, and then he threatened to excommunicate me. All the old tricks. But I held firm.

AGNES. And thanks to whom?

CHARLES. Thanks to Agnes. We had rehearsed the whole scene in bed.

AGNES (*rising and crossing to* C) Well, then, my darling, if I have helped you with the Archbishop, you can surely buy me the new steeple-hat, and one for your little Queen, too—(*she moves above the rostrum* LC) because you have said some very hurtful things to her, without noticing it, as usual, you bad boy.

CHARLES (*overcome*) All right, then, order your steeple-hats.

(AGNES *crosses to* C)

I always have to say "Yes" to somebody; if it isn't the Archbishop, it's you. But I may as well tell you, I haven't the least idea how I'm going to pay for them.

AGNES. You're going to sign a draft on the Treasury, Charles, and we will see what happens later. (*To the Queen*) Come along, little Majesty.

(*The* QUEEN *rises*)

We will try them on together. Would you rather have this rose-coloured one, or the sky-blue? I think myself the rose is the one which will suit you best.

(AGNES *takes the* QUEEN's *hand and leads her up* C. "*Cuckoo*" *music is heard*)

CHARLES. What do you mean?

(AGNES *and the* QUEEN *stop and look at Charles*)

Have you got them already?

AGNES (*coming down a little*) You're very slow at understanding, my dearest. Surely you can see, if we were to have them in time for the ball we had to order them a month ago? But we were so sure you would say "Yes", weren't we, Your Majesty? (*She moves behind the fence* LC) You shall see what a sensation this causes in London. It's a great victory for France, you know, Charles.

(AGNES *and the* QUEEN *take to their heels and exit, laughing,* LC)

CHARLES (*sitting back on his throne*) There's nothing you can do but laugh, the way they harp on victories. La Tremouille, Dunois, they're all the same. There is always going to be a great victory. But everything has to be paid for, including great victories these days. And supposing I can't afford a great victory? Suppose France is above my means? (*He sits on the upstage arm of the throne, opens the seat box with his foot, and takes out an inkwell, paper and pen*) Ah well, we shall see. (*He puts his book in the seat box and closes it*) I can always sign a draft on the Treasury. Let's hope it will please the tradesmen. The Treasury is empty, but there's nothing on this paper to say so. (*He rises and crosses to* RC) You wouldn't like a steeple-hat, too, while I'm doing it? You needn't mind saying so. My signature isn't worth the ink it's written in. (*He kneels on the floor down* L *of the rostrum* RC *and writes*)

YOLANDE. I'm past the age for steeple-hats, Charles. I want something else.

CHARLES (*wearily*) To make me a great King, I know. It gets very boring in the end; everybody wants to make me a great King. Even Agnes. Even in bed. Imagine how jolly that is. I wish you would all try and get it into your heads, I'm an unimportant, insignificant Valois—(*he signs his name on the paper*) and to make a King of me would need a miracle. I know my grandfather Charles was a great King; but he lived before the war when everything was much cheaper. Besides, he was rich. But my father and mother spent it all, so whether you like it or not, I can't afford to be a great King; I haven't got the money, and I haven't got the courage; you all know I haven't. Courage is far too dangerous in a world full of bullying brutes. That fat pig La Tremouille was in a roaring temper the other day, and drew his sword on me. (*He rises and goes on to the rostrum* LC) We were alone together: nobody there to defend me. He was quite prepared to give me a jab with it, the beastly hooligan. I only just had time to dodge behind the throne. So you see what we've come to. Drawing his sword on the King. I should have sent for the constable to arrest him, except that unfortunately he is the constable, and I'm not so sure that I am the King. That's why they treat me like this; they know that I may be only a bastard. (*He puts the paper, pen and inkwell into the throne seat box, closes it and picks up his cup-and-ball*)

YOLANDE. It's nobody but yourself, Charles, who is always saying so.

CHARLES. When I look at all the legitimate faces about me—I hope I am a bastard. It's a charming day and age to live in, when a man isn't considered anybody unless he can brandish an eight-pound sword, and stroll about in a suit of armour which would sink a galleon. When they put it on me, I'm welded into the ground; a great help to my dignity and I don't like fighting. I don't like hitting, and I don't like being hit. And what's more, if you want to know, I'm frightened of it. (*He turns towards Yolande. Crossly*) What other impossibilities do you want me to do? (*He sits on the upstage arm of his throne, with his feet on the seat*)

YOLANDE (*rising*) I want you to receive this girl from Vaucouleurs. (*She crosses to* C. *Gently*) I think a peasant in your counsels is exactly what you all need. The nobility governs the kingdom, which is as it should be; God has entrusted it into their hands.

(*She moves* LC)   But, without presuming to criticize the wisdom of providence, I wonder sometimes that he hasn't given them what he gives so generously to humbler men, a better measure of simplicity and common sense.

CHARLES (*ironically*) And courage.

YOLANDE (*gently*) And courage, Charles.

CHARLES. As far as I can understand you, you recommend turning the government over to the people? To the good people who have all the virtues. You've read the history of tyrants, I suppose?

YOLANDE. No, Charles. In my day, knowledge was not encouraged in young women.

CHARLES. But I've read it: the endless procession of horrors and scandals; and I amuse myself sometimes by imagining how the procession will go on in the future. (*He sits on the throne and puts his legs over the downstage arm*) They will certainly try what you recommend. They'll try everything. Men of the people will become masters of the kingdoms, maybe for centuries, the time it takes for a meteor to cross the sky; and that will be the time for massacres and the most monstrous errors. And what will they find, at the great account, when all is done? They'll find that not even the most vile, capricious, and cruel of the princes have cost the world as much as one of these virtuous men. Give France a powerful man of action, born of the people, whose ambition is to make the people happy, whatever it may entail, and see how they'll come to wish to God they had their poor lazy Charles back again, with his everlasting games of cup-and-ball. At least I've no theories about organizing the happy life. A negative virtue, perhaps, but more valuable than they realize yet. (*He plays with his cup-and-ball*)

YOLANDE. You should give up this cup-and-ball game, Charles, and this habit of sitting upside down on your throne. It's no behaviour for a King. (*She crosses below the rostrum* LC *and stands down* L)

CHARLES. You would be sensible to let me be as I am. When the ball misses the cup, it drops on to my nose and nobody else's. But sit me on the throne the right way up, with the Orb in one hand and the Sceptre in the other, taking myself seriously, then whenever I make a mistake the ball will drop on to everybody's nose.

(*The* ARCHBISHOP OF RHEIMS *and* M. DE LA TREMOUILLE *enter up* R *and cross to* C. CHARLES *sits like a king on his throne*)

Archbishop, Constable, you've come at the perfect moment. I am starting to govern. You see I have here the Orb and Sceptre.

ARCHBISHOP (*taking his eyeglass*) It's a cup-and-ball.

(TREMOUILLE *stands* R *of the Archbishop*)

CHARLES. Unimportant, Archbishop; symbolism, after all. That isn't something I have to teach a prince of the Church. You come in unannounced, my lord, do you wish for an audience?

ARCHBISHOP. I haven't come to be playful, Sire. I know very well the minority opinion, which cares to intrigue and agitate on every possible occasion, is trying to persuade you to see this notorious peasant girl you have heard of. The Constable and I are here, Sire, to say it is not our intention to admit her.

(TREMOUILLE *grunts agreement*)

CHARLES (*to Yolande*) What did I tell you? I have taken note of what you recommend, my lord, and I shall consider what course to follow. Now you may go; the audience is over.

ARCHBISHOP. I will remind you, Sire, we are not here for your amusement.

CHARLES. Whenever I talk like a king for a moment, they always think I'm amusing myself. (*He lies back on his throne with the cup-and-ball*) Very well, then, leave me to amuse myself in peace. (*He puts his legs over the downstage arm*)

ARCHBISHOP. This girl's miraculous reputation is spreading across the country ahead of her; it was here before she arrived; it's already causing excitement in besieged Orleans. A soldier called her I don't know what when she arrived at Chinon. She told him that he was wrong to swear, because soon he would be standing before his Redeemer. And an hour later this boorish fellow missed his footing, and fell into the well in the servants' yard, and drowned himself. That blundering step of a drunkard has done more for this girl's reputation than a great victory ever did for Dunois. Apparently, the opinion is unanimous, from the lowest kennel-boy to the highest lady in your court: only this wretched girl can save us. A preposterous infatuation.

(CHARLES *plays with his cup-and-ball*)

I speak to you, sir, of the gravest matters of the realm, and you play at cup-and-ball.

CHARLES. My lord, let us be clear about this. Do you want me to play at cup-and-ball, or do you want me to govern? (*He sits up*) Do you want me to govern?

ARCHBISHOP (*disturbed*) Sir, we don't ask you to go as far as that. We wish you to notice and appreciate the efforts we are making . . .

CHARLES. I assure you, ' notice them; I appreciate them; and I find them quite useless, my lord. Everyone expects me to see this girl; isn't it so?

ARCHBISHOP. I haven't said that.

CHARLES. Well, for my own part, I'm not at all curious to see her. I'm not fond of new faces; we have to know too many people as it is. And messengers from God aren't usually very enlivening.

But I want to be a good King, and content my people. (*He rises*) I shall see this peasant girl, if only to take the wind out of her sails. (*He crosses slowly to* R) And if she can make me want to listen to her talking about the welfare of the kingdom, which no-one has ever done yet without making me yawn, then there's no doubt about her performing miracles.

ARCHBISHOP (*muttering*) A peasant girl in the presence of the King.

TREMOUILLE. Disgraceful!

CHARLES (*stepping on to the rostrum* RC; *simply*) You will remember, I think, that some of all kinds have been admitted to my presence. (*He dangles his cup-and-ball in front of Tremouille's face*)

(TREMOUILLE *is furious*)

I don't mean M. de la Tremouille, who springs, of course, direct from Jupiter's thigh. But, for instance, yourself, my lord: I think I remember being told you were the grandson of a wine merchant. There is no reproach in that. What could be more natural? (*He crosses to* L *of the Archbishop*) You carried your own wine from the cellar to the altar. And as for myself, as you frequently have told me, it's a moot point whether I'm the son of a King. So we'd better not play the ancestry game, my lord, or we shall be making ourselves altogether ridiculous. (*He laughs, moves to Yolande, takes her hand and leads her up* C) Come with me, and help me get ready for her.

(*The* ARCHBISHOP *moves* RC)

I've thought of a very amusing joke. We can disguise one of the pages in a royal doublet, if we can find one that isn't too shabby; sit him on the throne—(*he leads Yolande behind the fence* LC) which I am sure he will manage better than I can, and I shall hide myself in the crowd. Then we can listen to a solemn harangue from the messenger of God to a page-boy. It ought to be irresistible; don't you think so?

(CHARLES *and* YOLANDE *exit* LC)

ARCHBISHOP. Do we let him do it? It's a game to him, like everything else. (*He sits on the downstage end of the rostrum* RC) It shouldn't be dangerous.

TREMOUILLE (*moving to* L *of the Archbishop*) I command the army, Archbishop, and I can only tell you, the official doctor of the nation has nothing more to say. We're now entirely in the hands of the bone-setters, the faith-healers, the quacks. In other words, what you call messengers from God. What do we risk? (*He sits* L *of the Archbishop*)

ARCHBISHOP (*anxiously*) With God everything is always a risk. Long experience as a man, both in the church and in government, teaches me that never, never must we draw God's attention to us. It is better to remain very small, Constable, very small and unnoticed.

(TREMOUILLE *and the* ARCHBISHOP *rise.*

EVERYONE *enters, chattering loudly. The* PAGE TO THE DAUPHIN *enters down* L *and sits on the throne.* CAUCHON *and the* INQUISITOR *enter* LC *and stand on the rostrum* LC. CAPTAIN LA HIRE *enters down* L *and stands below the throne.* FATHER, MOTHER *and* BROTHER *enter down* R *and stand down* R. WARWICK *and the* PRO-MOTER *enter up* R *and stand up* C. BEAUDRICOURT *and* LADVENU *enter* RC *and stand up* RC. YOLANDE *enters up* L *and stands above the throne. The* QUEEN *and* AGNES *enter* RC *and stand on the rostrum* RC. *Two* SOLDIERS *enter up* R *and stand up* C. CHARLES *enters* RC *and stands* L *of Agnes, talking to her.*

JOAN, *escorted by a* SOLDIER, *enters up* R *and moves down* C. BEAUDRICOURT *claps his hands for silence. It is quiet as* JOAN *comes down* C, *looking round. She sees the throne and is about to kneel when she stops and looks at the Page)*

YOLANDE. You must kneel, child, before the King.

(JOAN *looks around and crosses slowly down* R. *As she does so,* CHARLES *goes round the back of the throne to* R *of La Hire down* L, *and talks to him.* JOAN *sees the back of Charles. There is a pause, then* CHARLES *turns as* JOAN *approaches him. There are loud murmurs, and the* ARCHBISHOP *quietens everyone with a gesture.* JOAN *kneels at Charles' feet and clasps his legs. The* SOLDIER *escorting Joan, moves up* C)

CHARLES (*embarrassed in the silence*) What do you want with me, mademoiselle?

JOAN. Gentle Dauphin, I am called "Joan the Maid". God has brought me to you, to tell you that you will be anointed and crowned in the city of Rheims. You will be viceroy of the King of Heaven, who is King of France.

CHARLES (*awkwardly*) Well, that is very nice, mademoiselle. But Rheims belongs to the English, I understand. How would I get there?

JOAN (*still on her knees*) By your own strength, gentle Dauphin; by beating them. We will start with Orleans, and then we can go to Rheims.

(*The* COURTIERS *react*)

CHARLES. How did you recognize me without my crown?

JOAN (*rising*) Gentle Dauphin, it was a good joke to put your crown on this boy, but it doesn't take much to see that he's really a little nobody.

(*The* PAGE *reacts*)

CHARLES. You're mistaken, mademoiselle. The boy is the son of a great lord.

JOAN. Great lords are not the King.

CHARLES (*troubled*) Who told you I was the King? I don't look like a king.

JOAN (*taking his hand*) God told me, gentle Dauphin: who appointed you from the beginning of time, through your father and your grandfather and all the line of kings, to be viceroy of his kingdom.

CHARLES. Interesting—remarkable. (*He signals to the Page to get off the throne*)

(*The* PAGE *rises and goes down* L. *The* ARCHBISHOP *and* TRE-MOUILLE *exchange looks of annoyance. There are general murmurs from the crowd.* CHARLES *signals Joan to cross to his left.* JOAN *crosses to* L *of Charles*)

ARCHBISHOP (*moving* C) Sire. In a matter as delicate as this, you cannot surround yourself with precautions too strict or thorough.

(CHARLES *moves to the throne and sits*)

A commission of learned theologians must question and examine her very closely. We will then discuss their report in Council, and decide if it is necessary for you to give this girl a longer hearing. There's no need for her to importune you any further today. I shall myself interrogate her first of all. Come here, my daughter. (*He beckons to Joan*)

CHARLES. Not at all. (*He stops Joan*) Stay where you are. (*He turns to the Archbishop, taking Joan's hand to give himself courage*) I was the one she recognized. I was the one she spoke to. I wish you to leave me alone with her: all of you.

(*There is a gasp from everyone*)

ARCHBISHOP. This blunt dismissal, sir: it is quite extraordinary.

TREMOUILLE. Extraordinary!

ARCHBISHOP. It is improper. Apart from all else, you should at least think of your own security.

(CHARLES *is fearful for a moment, but looks at Joan and pulls him-self together*)

CHARLES. I am the only judge of that. (*He recites*) Through my father, my grandfather, and all the line of kings . . . (*He winks at Joan*) Isn't that right? (*He turns imperturbably to the others*) Leave us, my lords, when the King commands it.

(*The* COURTIERS *all bow and exit*)

(*He keeps his regal pose for a moment, then explodes with laughter, rises and moves* C, *looking off* R *and* L) They've gone, they've gone. Did

I do that—(*he moves down* RC) or did you? It's the first time in my life I have ever made myself obeyed. (*He looks at Joan, suddenly anxious*) I hope there is nothing in what the Archbishop was trying to suggest. You haven't come here to kill me? There isn't a knife hidden about you somewhere?

(JOAN *smiles gravely*)

No. You reassure me. I had forgotten, among all these pirates in my court, how reassuring a smile could be. Are there many of you in my kingdom with such honest faces?

JOAN (*still smiling gravely*) Yes, sir, very many.

CHARLES. But I never see you. Only ruffians, hypocrites, and whores: my entourage. (*He sits on the rostrum* RC) Though of course there's my little Queen, who has a certain amount of charm but not many brains. Well, there you are. I suppose now you have to start boring me. You're going to tell me to become a great King.

JOAN (*crossing to* C; *gently*) Yes, Sire.

CHARLES. Don't let's bother. We shall have to stay shut up here together for an hour at least, to impress them. If you talk to me about God and the kingdom of France for an hour, I shall never last out. I propose instead we talk about something quite different. Do you play cards? (*He rises and moves to* R *of Joan*)

JOAN (*opening her eyes wide*) I don't know what it is.

CHARLES. It's an amusing game they invented for Papa, to distract him during his illness. You'll see, I shall teach you. (*He crosses below Joan to the throne*) I've played so often now I've got tired of it, but I think you may like it if you've never played before. (*He opens the throne box and rummages inside*) I hope they haven't stolen them from me. They steal everything here.

(JOAN *moves* LC)

And a pack of cards, you know, costs a lot of money. Only the royal princes have them. Mine were left to me by my father. I shall never have enough money to buy myself another pack. If those devils have stolen them . . . (*He finds the cards*) No, here they are. (*He sits on the edge of the rostrum* LC, *in front of the throne*) You knew Papa was mad, did you? Sometimes I hope I'm really his son, so that I can be sure I'm the true King; and then, at other times I hope I'm a bastard, so that I don't have to dread going mad before I'm thirty. (*He shuffles the cards*)

JOAN (*gently*) And which of the two would you prefer, Charles?

CHARLES (*rising; surprised*) Good heavens, are you calling me Charles? (*He sits on the throne*) This is turning out to be a most surprising day. I believe I'm not going to be bored, for once; it's astonishing.

JOAN. Not now, Charles, or ever again.

CHARLES. Really astonishing. Which of the two would I

prefer? Well, I suppose on the days when I have some courage I would rather take the risk of going mad, and be the true King; and on the days when I haven't I would rather let everything go, and retire on my twopence-ha'penny to somewhere abroad, and live in peace.

JOAN (*suddenly grave*) And today, are you feeling brave today, Charles?

CHARLES. Today? (*He ponders a moment*) Yes, it seems to me I feel fairly brave. Not very, but fairly. Well, you saw how I packed off the Archbishop.

JOAN. How would you like to be brave all the time, from today onwards? (*She steps on to the rostrum and stands above the throne*)

CHARLES (*leaning forward; interested*) Do you really mean you know the secret?

JOAN. Yes.

CHARLES. Would you sell it to me, without letting the others know about it? I'm not very well off, but I could make you a draft on the Treasury.

JOAN. I will give it to you, Charles.

CHARLES (*suspiciously*) For nothing?

JOAN. Yes.

CHARLES. Then I'm not interested. A secret is either no good, or far beyond my means. Disinterested people are too rare, at any price. I've taken to behaving like a fool, so that I shall be left in peace, but I know more than you think I know. I'm not so easily gulled.

JOAN. You know too much.

CHARLES. Too much? You can never know too much.

JOAN. Sometimes; it is possible.

CHARLES. I have to defend myself. You would soon see, if you were here in my position. If you were alone, among a lot of brutes whose one idea is to stab you when you are least expecting it, and if you've been born a weak sort of fellow, as I was—(*he rises*) you would soon—(*he crosses down* RC) realize the only way to steer safely through it is by being more clever than they are. And I am; much more clever. Which is why I more or less hang on to my throne.

JOAN. I shall be with you now, defending you.

CHARLES. Do you think you will?

JOAN. And I'm strong. I'm not afraid.

CHARLES (*sighing*) You're very lucky. Come on, I'm going to teach you to play cards. (*He kneels on the floor down* RC)

JOAN (*crossing and kneeling* L *of Charles; smiling*) All right. And then I'll teach you something.

CHARLES. What?

JOAN. Not to be afraid. And not to know too much.

CHARLES. Now pay attention. You see the cards, and these pictures on them? There's something of everything here—(*he shows her the cards*) knaves, queens, kings: the same as in the world: and here are the commoners: spades, hearts, clubs, diamonds. Those are the troops. There are plenty of them; you can lose as many as you like. (*He deals three cards each*) You deal the cards without looking at them, and fate either gives you a good hand, or a bad hand, and then the battle begins. (*He motions to Joan to pick up her cards*)

(JOAN *picks up her cards*)

(*He looks at his hand, then at Joan's, and exchanges one of his cards for one of her's*) The higher cards can capture the lower cards.

(*They play twice*, CHARLES *winning each time*)

(*He points to their two remaining cards. He has an ace, Joan a king*) Which do you think is the strongest?

JOAN. The king is.

CHARLES. Well, he is almost the strongest, but there's one stronger still. This card here, for instance, the single heart. Do you know what it's called?

JOAN. God. He's the only one who commands kings.

CHARLES (*annoyed*) For goodness sake let God alone for five minutes. For the time being we're playing cards. It's called the ace.

JOAN (*throwing her card down*) Then the game of cards is ridiculous. What can be stronger than a king, except God?

CHARLES. The ace, in fact. You're not so intelligent as I thought. The ace, or God if you like; but there's one in each camp. (*He finds the four aces*) You see: ace of hearts, ace of spades, ace of clubs, ace of diamonds. One for each of them. Do you think the English don't say their prayers, as well as us? And, what's more, to a God who protects them, and gives them victories over us. And my cousin, the Duke of Burgundy, he has a God for Burgundy, in just the same way: a smallish one, maybe, but a bold one, a cunning one, who gets my cousin out of difficulties very well. God is with everybody, my girl. (*He gathers the cards into a pile*) But, in the long run, He plumps for the people who have the most money and the biggest armies. So why do you imagine He should be with France, now that France has got nothing at all? (*He picks up the cards*)

JOAN. Perhaps for that reason: because she has nothing at all, Charles.

CHARLES (*shrugging his shoulders*) You don't know Him.

JOAN. God isn't with the strongest; He is with the bravest. There's the difference. God hasn't any love for cowards.

CHARLES. Then he doesn't love me. (*He rises*) And if He doesn't love me, why do you expect me to love Him? All He had to do was to give me some courage. I don't ask for anything better.

JOAN (*rising; severely*) Do you think He's your nurse, with no-one else to think about but you? Why don't you make the best of what you've got? It's true He made you a bit weak in the leg . . .

CHARLES (*crossing below Joan to* C) You've noticed that? He ought to have managed better than that. Particularly with the present fashions. It's because of my legs that Agnes can't bring herself to love me. If He had only an eye for proportion, and hadn't given me big knees as well . . . (*He goes on to the rostrum* LC *and puts the cards in the box*)

JOAN. Well, I grant you that. He didn't go to much trouble over your knees. (*She moves* LC) But there was something else that more concerned Him; His eye was on your head and your heart, Charles, where you most resemble Him. And there it is He makes you free, to be whatever you will.

(CHARLES *crosses down* R, *then turns and moves a little up* C)

You can use them to play cards, or to outmanœuvre the Archbishop for a time, though in the end you have to pay for it—(*she moves to* L *of Charles*) or else you can use them to make the house of Valois glorious again. Your little Queen gave you a son, Charles. What are you going to leave the boy when you die? This wretched scrap of France, nibbled by the English? If so, when he grows up, the boy will be able to say, as you did just now, that God hasn't any interest in him. You, Charles, are God to your little son; and you have to take care of him.

CHARLES (*with a step towards her; groaning*) But I keep telling you, everything frightens me.

(JOAN *takes Charles' hand. They both sit on the rostrum* RC, JOAN L *of* CHARLES)

JOAN. You shall have the secret now, Charles. But don't give me away when I tell you first that everything frightens me, too. Do you know why M. de la Tremouille isn't afraid of anything?

CHARLES. Because he is strong.

JOAN. No. Because he is stupid. He never imagines anything. Wild boars and bulls are never afraid of anything, either. And I tell you this: it has been even more complicated for me to get to you than it will be for you to get to Orleans and refashion your kingdom. I had to explain to my father, and, my goodness, the English don't hit any harder than he does. And then I had to make my mother cry; there was nothing worse than that; and then to convince Beaudricourt, who didn't want to think of anything except adding one more to his sins. Don't think I haven't been afraid. I was afraid all the time, from the very beginning.

CHARLES. Then how have you done it?

JOAN. Just as I should have done without the fear. That's all the difficulty there is, Charles. Try it once, and see. You say: one thing is obvious, I'm frightened, which is nobody's business but mine, and now on I go. And on you go. And if you see something ahead which nothing you know about yourself can overcome . . .

CHARLES. Like Tremouille in one of his rages.

JOAN. Yes, if you like. Or the unshakable English facing Orleans in their fortress built like rocks. You say: Here it is— they outnumber us, their walls are as thick as the length of a giant's arm, their cannons out-thunder thunder, their arrows out-rain the rain. So be it. I'm frightened. Now I've realized how frightening it is, on we go. And the English are so astonished they begin to be frightened themselves, and you get through. You get through because you think deeper, imagine more, and get your fear over first. That's the secret of it.

CHARLES. But is it always so successful?

JOAN. Always. As long as you turn and face what frightens you.

CHARLES (*after a pause*) You think we could try your secret?

JOAN. We have to try it.

CHARLES (*suddenly frightened by his temerity*) Tomorrow, perhaps. By tomorrow I shall have had time to prepare for it.

JOAN. Now, Charles, now. You are ready now.

CHARLES. Do you mean that I'm ready to call the Archbishop and La Tremouille? That I'm ready to tell them that I've given you command of the army, and then to sit calmly back and watch their faces?

JOAN. Absolutely ready.

CHARLES (*rising and crossing to* LC) I'm scared out of my wits.

JOAN (*rising and crossing to* R *of Charles*) Then the worst is over. The whole thing is to be frightened first. One thing is essential: you mustn't be still frightened after you've called them. Are you sure you are as frightened now as you possibly can be?

CHARLES (*his hand on his belly*) Oh, yes, I agree with you. (*Doubled up, he makes a circle around her*)

JOAN. Wonderful! That's an enormous advantage. When they start to be frightened, you will have got over it already. The whole scheme is to be afraid first, before the battle begins. (*She holds him up*) You'll soon see. I'll call them. (*She moves up* C *and calls*) My lord Archbishop, M. de la Tremouille, everyone. M. le Dauphin wishes to speak to you.

CHARLES (*moving about* LC; *taken by panic*) Oh, dear, I'm so frightened. Goodness, goodness, I'm frightened.

JOAN (*moving down* C) That's right, Charles, more frightened still.

CHARLES (*his teeth chattering*) I can't be more frightened, it's impossible. (*He collapses against his throne*)

JOAN. Then we have the victory. (*She moves above the rostrum* LC) God has joined you; He says, "Charles is afraid, but still he calls them". In eight hours we shall hold Orleans.

(*The* ARCHBISHOP *and* TREMOUILLE, *surprised, enter up* R *and move down* C. *They are followed by the full company. The* INQUISITOR *and the* PROMOTER *stand on the rostrum* LC. CAUCHON *and* WARWICK *stand behind the fence up* R. YOLANDE *stands above the throne* LC. AGNES *and the* QUEEN *stand on the rostrum* RC. *The* PAGE *stands down* L *below the throne.* LA HIRE *stands down* R. FATHER, MOTHER *and* BROTHER *stand behind the fence* LC. BEAUDRICOURT *and* LADVENU *stand up* RC. *The* SOLDIERS *stand in a line at the back.*)

ARCHBISHOP. You called us, Your Highness?

CHARLES (*suddenly; after a last look at* Joan) Yes: I've come to a decision, my lord, and it also concerns you, M. de la Tremouille. (*He rises and stands on the seat of his throne*) I am giving the command of my royal army to this Maid here.

(TREMOUILLE *is about to speak*)

(*He suddenly shouts*) If you don't agree, M. de la Tremouille, I must ask you to surrender your sword to me. You are under arrest!

(TREMOUILLE *and the* ARCHBISHOP *stand petrified*)

JOAN (*clapping her hands*) Well done! Now you know how simple it is. Do you see their faces, Charles? Look at them: do look at them. Who is frightened now, Charles? (*She bursts out laughing*)

(CHARLES *begins to laugh as well. They rock with laughter, unable to stop, and the* ARCHBISHOP *and* TREMOUILLE *seem turned to stone*)

(*She suddenly drops on to her knees down* LC, *crying*) Thank you, God!

CHARLES (*kneeling on the rostrum*) On to your knees, M. de la Tremouille, on to your knees.

(TREMOUILLE, *stupefied by the blow, falls to his knees.* "Horse" *music is heard*)

And give us your blessing, Archbishop: no hesitating: give us your blessing. Now that we've all been thoroughly frightened, we must make straight for Orleans.

Everyone slowly kneels. The ARCHBISHOP, *bewildered, mechanically gives his blessing as—*

the CURTAIN *quickly falls*

PART II

The setting is the same as at the beginning of Part I. See Ground Plan A.

When the CURTAIN *rises, the* ARCHBISHOP *and* TREMOUILLE *are kneeling down* C, *the* ARCHBISHOP R *of Tremouille.* JOAN *is kneeling down* LC, *with* CHARLES *kneeling* L *of her. The* PROMOTER *is standing at the left end of the fence up* RC. LADVENU *is standing behind the fence up* C. *The* INQUISITOR *is sitting on the top step of the rostrums* LC. WARWICK *and* CAUCHON *enter up* R *and stand behind the fence down* R.

WARWICK (*laughing*) In point of fact, that wasn't exactly how it happened. They called a meeting of the Council, and discussed the matter for hours. In the end they agreed to use Joan as a sort of flagpole to nail their colours to: an attractive little mascot, well qualified to charm the general public into letting themselves be killed. The best we could do to restore the balance was to treble the men's drink ration before they went into action, though it had nothing like as good an effect. (*He moves* L *of the fence and comes down* R)

(CAUCHON *follows Warwick and stands* L *of him*)

We started being beaten from that time on, against all the laws of strategy. I know some people have said there was nothing miraculous in that. They maintain that our system of isolated forts around Orleans was ludicrous, and all the enemy had to do was attack: which is what Joan made them agree to try. But that's not true. Sir John Talbot was no fool. He knew his job thoroughly well. His system of fortification was theoretically impregnable. No: we must have the grace to admit, there was more in it than that: a strong element of imponderable—or God, as you might say, my lord Bishop—which the rules of strategy don't provide for. Without question, it was Joan—(*he crosses below* Joan *to* L *of her*) singing like a lark in the sky over the heads of your French armies on the march. (*He moves behind* Joan) I am very fond of France, my lord: which is why I should be most unhappy if we lost her. This lark singing in the sky, while we all take aim to shoot her down: that seems very like France to me. Or at least like the best of her. In her time she has had plenty of fools—(*he points at the Archbishop with his stick*) rogues and blunderers; but every now and then a lark sings in her sky, and the fools and the rogues—(*he crosses to* L *of Cauchon*) can be forgotten. I am very fond of France.

CAUCHON (*gently*) But still you take aim and shoot her down.

WARWICK. A man is a mass of contradictions, my lord Bishop. It isn't unusual in him to kill what he loves. I love animals, but I hunt them, too. (*He suddenly raps with his stick on his boot*) Come along now: the lark has been caught. The cage of Compeigne——

(CHARLES, *the* ARCHBISHOP *and* TREMOUILLE *rise and slyly edge behind the fence down* R, *away from Joan*)

—has shut her in. The singing is over; and Charles and his court are leaving her there, without a second glance. (*He moves up* C) They're going back to their old political method, now that their little mascot isn't bringing them luck any more.

(JOAN *rises and moves towards Charles.* CAUCHON *gets between Joan and Charles*)

CAUCHON. Your King has left you, Joan. There's no reason now to go on defending him. Yesterday we read you the letter he has sent to every town, telling them to say he repudiates you.

JOAN (*after a pause; quietly*) He is my King. (*She moves to the stool down* C *and sits*)

CHARLES (*to the Archbishop; in a low voice*) That letter is going to be thrown in your teeth for a long time yet.

(CAUCHON *crosses to the rostrum* LC *and stands on the first step*)

ARCHBISHOP (*also aside*) It had to be, sir; it was absolutely necessary. At this juncture, the cause of France cannot be linked in any way with Joan's.

CAUCHON. Joan: listen carefully, and try to understand what I'm saying. Your King is not our King. A treaty in rightful and due form has made Henry the Sixth of Lancaster King of France and England. The useless resistance of the man you call your King, and his absurd pretensions to a throne which isn't his, appear to us to be acts of rebellion and terrorism against a peace which was almost assured. The puppet whom you served is not our master, be certain of that. (*He sits on the second step of the rostrum*)

JOAN. Say what you like, you can't alter the truth. That is the King God gave you, with his weak legs and his bony knees.

CHARLES (*to the Archbishop*) This is really most disagreeable.

ARCHBISHOP. For a little while we have to have patience; but they mean to hurry through the trial and burn her, and after that we shall not be disturbed. You must surely admit, sir, the English have done us a good turn, making themselves responsible for this arrest and execution. If they hadn't done it, we ourselves should have had to, some day or other. She was becoming impossible.

(CHARLES, *the* ARCHBISHOP *and* TREMOUILLE *exit unnoticed down* R. *The* PROMOTER *moves and stands behind the fence down* R)

CAUCHON. We know by many of your answers, insolent though they were, that you're not slow of understanding, Joan.

Put yourself for a moment in our place. Do you really expect us, with most earnest human convictions, to believe that God has sent you to oppose the cause we defend? How can you think, only because you say Voices have spoken to you, that we should believe God to be against us.

JOAN. You will know when we have beaten you.

CAUCHON (*shrugging*) You are answering like a self-willed, obstinate child. Do you think you are the first who has heard Voices?

JOAN. No, of course not.

CAUCHON. Neither the first, nor the last, Joan. Now, do you believe that each time a little girl goes to her village priest and says: "I have seen some saint, or the Blessed Virgin, I have heard Voices which have told me to do one thing or another"—that her priest should believe and encourage her: and how long then would the church still remain?

JOAN. I don't know.

CAUCHON. You don't know; but you are full of good sense, and that is why I am trying to lead you to reason with me. Have you not been in command in battle, Joan? (*He rises and stands at the foot of the rostrum*)

JOAN. Yes, I was in command of hundreds of good soldiers who followed me, and believed me.

CAUCHON (*sitting on the bottom step of the rostrum*) You were in command. And if on the morning of some attack one of your soldiers had heard Voices persuading him to attack by another gate than the one you had chosen, or not to attack at all, what would you have done?

(JOAN *is speechless for a moment, then she suddenly bursts out laughing*)

JOAN. My lord Bishop, it's easy to see you're a priest. It's clear you don't know much about our men. They can drink, and swear and fight, but they're not ones for hearing Voices.

CAUCHON. A joke is no answer, Joan. But you gave your answer before you spoke, in the second of hesitation when you were held and arrested by what I said to you. (*He rises and crosses to L of Joan*) And you see it is true: that the church militant is an army in a world still overrun by infidels and the powers of evil. The church owes obedience to our Holy Father the Pope and his bishops, as your soldiers owed obedience to you and your lieutenants. If a soldier says on the morning of attack that Voices have told him not to advance, in yours or any army in the world, he would be silenced. And far more brutally than this effort of ours to reason with you.

JOAN (*gathering herself together; on the defensive*) You have a right to hit at me with all your power. And my right is to say "No", and go on believing.

CAUCHON (*crossing above Joan to* R *of her*) Don't make yourself a prisoner of your own pride, Joan. You can surely see that we have no possible reason, either as men or as priests, to believe that your mission is divinely inspired. You alone have a reason to believe so; encouraged in that belief by the fiend who means to damn you, and also as long as you were useful to them, by those whom you served. You served them; and yet the way they behaved before your capture, and their explicit repudiation since, certainly proves that the most intelligent of them never believed you. (*He moves down* R) No-one believes you, Joan, any longer, except the common people, who believe anything, and tomorrow they will believe half a dozen others. You are quite alone.

(JOAN *makes no reply, sitting small and quiet among them all*)

(*He crosses above Joan to* L *of her*) I beg you not to imagine that your strong will and your stubborn resistance to us is a sign that God is upholding you. The devil has also got intelligence and a tough hide. His mind had the flash of a star among the angels before he rebelled.

JOAN (*after a pause*) I am not intelligent, my lord. I am a peasant girl, the same as any other in my village. But when something is black I cannot say it is white, that is all.

(*There is a pause.* CAUCHON *sits on the bottom step of the rostrum* LC)

PROMOTER (*moving to* R *of Joan*) What was the sign you gave to the man you are calling your King, to make him trust you with his army?

JOAN. I don't know what you mean: what sign I gave.

PROMOTER. Did you make him sip mandragora, to be a protection against harm?

(LADVENU *crosses to* L *of the fence down* R)

JOAN. I don't know what you mean by mandragora.

PROMOTER. Your secret has a name, whether it's a potion or a formula, and we mean to know it. What did you give him at Chinon to make him so heroic all of a sudden? A Hebrew name? The devil speaks all languages, but he delights in Hebrew.

JOAN (*smiling*) No, my lord: it has a French name. I gave him courage.

(*The* PROMOTER *moves down* R *of the fence down* R)

CAUCHON. And so you think that God, or at least the power you believe to be God, took no part in this?

JOAN. He takes part always, my lord Bishop. When a girl speaks two words of good sense and someone listens, God is there. But He is thrifty; when a ha'porth of good sense will do, He isn't likely to waste a miracle.

LADVENU (*quietly*) The answer's a good one, in all humility, my lord: it can't be held against her.

PROMOTER (*moving to* R *of Joan; with venom*) I see, I see!

(LADVENU *moves and stands up* L *of Joan*)

So you don't believe in such miracles as we are shown in the gospels? You deny what was done by Our Lord Jesus at the marriage of Cana? You deny that He raised Lazarus from the dead?

JOAN. No, my lord. What is written in Holy Scripture was surely done. He changed the water into wine just as easily as He created them. And it was no more difficult for Him the Master of life and death, to make Lazarus live again than for me to thread a needle.

PROMOTER (*crossing below Joan to* L *of her; yelping*) Listen to that! Listen to that! She says there is no such thing as a miracle.

(LADVENU *crosses to* R *of the fence down* R)

JOAN. No, my lord. I say that a true miracle is not done with a magic wand or incantation. The gipsies on our village green can do miracles of that sort. The true miracle is done by man alone, with the mind and courage which God has given to him.

(*The* PROMOTER *moves and stands above the rostrum* LC)

CAUCHON (*rising and moving to* L *of Joan*) Are you measuring the gravity of your words, Joan? You seem to be telling us quite calmly that God's true miracle on earth is man, who is nothing but sin and error, blindness and futility . . .

JOAN. And strength, too, and courage, and light sometimes when he is deepest in sin. I have seen men during the battles . . .

LADVENU. My lord, Joan is talking to us in her rough and ready language about things which come instinctively from her heart, which may be wrong but are surely simple and genuine. Her thoughts are not so schooled that she can shape them to our way of argument. Perhaps by pressing her with questions we run the risk of making her say more than she meant, or something different from her belief.

CAUCHON (*crossing above Joan to* L *of Ladvenu*) Brother Ladvenu, we shall try and estimate as fairly as we can what part lack of skill plays in her answers. But our duty is to question her to the last point of doubt. So then, Joan—(*he moves down* RC) you excuse man all his faults, and think him one of God's greatest miracles, even the only one?

JOAN. Yes, my lord.

PROMOTER (*moving to* L *of Joan; yelping and beside himself*) It's blasphemy! Man is filth, lust, a nightmare of obscenity.

JOAN. Yes, my lord. He sins; he is evil enough. And then something happens: he may be coming out of a brothel, and suddenly he has thrown himself at the reins of a runaway horse to save some child he has never seen before, and with his bones all broke, he dies at peace.

PROMOTER. But he dies like an animal, without a priest, in the full damnation of sin.

JOAN. No, my lord; he dies in the light which was lighted within him when the world began. He believed as a man, both in doing evil and doing good, and God created him in that contradiction to make his difficult way.

INQUISITOR (*calmly*) Joan.

(CAUCHON *moves below the fence down* R. *The* PROMOTER *moves and stands in front of the fence up* R. LADVENU *moves behind the fence down* R)

I have let you speak throughout this trial, with scarcely a question to you. I wanted you to find your way clearly to your position. It has taken some time. The Promoter could see only the devil, the Bishop only the pride of a young girl intoxicated with success; I waited for something else to show itself. Now it has happened. (*He rises*) I represent the Holy Inquisition. My lord the Bishop told you just now, with great humanity, how his human feelings linked him with the English cause, which he considers just; and how they were confounded by his sentiments as priest and bishop, charged with the defence of our Mother Church. But I have come from the heart of Spain. This is the first time I have been sent to France. I know nothing of either the Armagnac faction, or of the English. It is indifferent to me who shall rule France, whether your prince or Henry of Lancaster. As for that strict discipline of our Mother Church which will not tolerate those who play a lone hand, however well-intentioned, but directs them back into the fold: I'll not say that is indifferent to me; but it is perhaps a secondary task, which the Inquisition leaves to the Bishops and the parish priests. The Holy Inquisition has something higher and more secret to defend. She wrestles on an invisible ground, inwardly, with an enemy only she knows how to detect, of whom only she can estimate the danger. It has been her care sometimes to take up arms against an Emperor; at other times the solemnity, the same vigilance, the same fixity of purpose have been deployed against some old apparently inoffensive scholar, or a herdsman buried away in a mountain village, or a young girl. The princes of the earth laugh very heartily to see the Inquisition give itself such endless care, when for them a piece of rope or a sergeant's signature on a death warrant would be enough. The Inquisition lets them laugh. It knows how to recognize the enemy; it knows better than to underestimate him wherever he may be found. And its enemy is not the devil, not the devil with the cloven hooves, the chastener of troublesome children, whom my lord Promoter sees on every side. Its enemy,

you yourself spoke his name, when at last you came into the open:
its only enemy, is man. Stand up, Joan, and answer me.

(JOAN *rises*)

I am your interrogator now.

(JOAN *turns towards the Inquisitor*)

(*In an expressionless voice*)   Are you a Christian?
    JOAN. Yes, my lord.
    INQUISITOR. You were baptized, and in your earliest years you
lived in the shadow of the church whose walls touched the walls
of your home. The church bells ruled over your day, your play-
time, your work, and your prayers. The emissaries we sent to
your village have all come back with the same story: you were a
little girl full of piety. Sometimes, instead of playing and running
about with other children, though you were not a solemn child,
you delighted to play, yet you would slip away into the church,
and for a long time you would be there alone, kneeling, not even
praying, but gazing at the coloured glass of the window.
    JOAN. Yes. I was happy there.
    INQUISITOR. You had a friend you loved very dearly, a little
girl called Haumette.
    JOAN. Yes, my lord.
    INQUISITOR. And when you made up your mind to leave for
Vaucouleurs, already believing that you would never go back,
you said good-bye to all your other friends, but you passed her
house by.
    JOAN. Yes. I was afraid to be too unhappy.
    INQUISITOR. But you cared for more than only those you loved
most. You cared for old people in sickness, children in poverty.
And later on, when you fought in your first battle, you stood
among the wounded and cried very bitterly.
    JOAN. French blood was being shed; it was hard to bear.
    INQUISITOR. Not only because it was French blood. A bully
who had captured two English soldiers in a skirmish outside
Orleans, knocked one of them down because he didn't move fast
enough for him. You jumped off your horse, took the man's head
on your knee, wiped the blood from his mouth, and helped him in
his dying, calling him your little son, and promising him Heaven.
    JOAN. How is it you can know that, my lord?
    INQUISITOR. The Inquisition knows everything, Joan. It
weighed your human tenderness in the scales before it sent me
to judge you.
    LADVENU. My lord Inquisitor, I am happy to hear you recal-
ling all these details which until now have been passed over in
silence. Yes, indeed, everything we know of Joan since her earliest
years has been gentleness, humility, and Christian charity.
    INQUISITOR (*turning on Ladvenu; suddenly stern*) Silence, Brother

Ladvenu. I ask you to remember that I stand here for the Holy Inquisition, alone qualified to make the distinction between Charity, the theological virtue, and the uncommendable, graceless, cloudy drink of the milk of human kindness. (*He passes his eye over them all*) Ah, my Masters! (*He resumes his seat*) How quickly your hearts can be melted. The accused has only to be a little girl, looking at you with a pair of wide-open eyes, and with a ha'porth of simple kindness, and you're all ready to fall over yourselves to absolve her. Very good guardians of the faith we have here. I see that the Holy Inquisition has enough on its plate still, and still it has to be cut away, cut, cut, always the dead wood to be cut away: and after us, others will go on, still pruning, hacking away without mercy, clearing the ranks of unruliness, so that the forest will be sound from root to branch.

(*There is a pause*)

LADVENU (*presently*) Our Saviour also loved with this loving-kindness, my lord. (*He crosses to the Inquisitor*) He said: "Suffer the little children to come unto me." He put His hand on the shoulder of the woman taken in adultery, and said to her, "Go in peace."

(*The* PROMOTER *moves to the right end of the fence up* C)

INQUISITOR. I tell you to be silent. Otherwise I shall have to investigate your case as well as Joan's. I see that we should have considered your age, and not your learning which I believe is remarkable, before we invited you to join us here. Experience will soon make plain to you that youth, generosity, human tenderness are names of the enemy. At least, I trust it may. Surely you can see, if we were so unwise as to put these words you have spoken into the minds of simple people, they would draw from them a love of Man. And love of Man excludes the love of God.

LADVENU (*quietly*) And yet He chose to become a man.

INQUISITOR (*rising and turning suddenly to Cauchon; curtly*) My lord Bishop, in virtue of your discretionary power as president of these debates, I ask you to dispense for today with the collaboration of your young assessor. I shall inform you, when the session is over, what conclusions will be entered against him, if needs be. (*He suddenly thunders*) Against him or against whomsoever. For no-one is of too great importance to be put out of your care: understand so. I would denounce myself, if God should allow me to be misled. (*He gravely crosses himself*) May He mercifully watch over me. (*He resumes his seat*)

(*A breath of fear whispers through the tribunal. The* PROMOTER *and* CAUCHON *cross themselves*)

CAUCHON (*with a gesture of distress to Ladvenu; simply*) Leave us, Brother Ladvenu.

LADVENU (*before he moves*) My lord Inquisitor, I owe you obedience, as I do my Reverend lord Bishop. I will go, saying no more—(*he takes a step up stage and turns*) except that my prayers must be to our Lord Jesus that He shall lead you to remember the fragility of your small enemy who faces you now.

(LADVENU *exits* LC. *The* PROMOTER *moves to the left end of the fence up* C. *The* INQUISITOR *does not speak until Ladvenu has gone*)

INQUISITOR (*quietly*) Small, fragile, tender, pure: and therefore formidable. (*He turns to Joan. In his neutral tone*) The first time you heard your Voices you were not yet fifteen. In fact you were a happy and contented little girl. And the unhappiness of France was only old men's talk. And yet one day you felt you should leave the village.

JOAN. My Voices told me that I must.

INQUISITOR. One day you felt that you must take upon yourself the unhappiness of others around you. And you knew even then everything that would come of it: how glorious your ride would be, how soon it would come to an end, and how once your king had been anointed, you would find yourself where you are now, surrounded and alone, the faggots heaped up in the market place, waiting to be set alight. This is the truth, and you know it.

JOAN. My Voices told me that I should be captured, and then delivered.

INQUISITOR. Delivered! They very well might use that word. Death is a deliverance, certainly. And you set off all the same, in spite of your father and mother, and in spite of all the grave difficulties ahead of you.

JOAN. Yes, my lord; it had to be. If I had been the daughter of a hundred mothers and a hundred fathers.

PROMOTER. Presumption! Pride! Don't you think you would have done better to go on with your sewing and spinning beside your mother?

JOAN. I had something else to do, my lord. There have always been plenty of women to do women's work.

(*The* PROMOTER *crosses and stands below the fence up* R)

INQUISITOR. Did it never occur to you to consecrate your life to prayer, supplicating Heaven to expel the English?

JOAN. God likes to see action first, my lord. Prayer is extra. (*She turns to Cauchon*) It was simpler to explain to Charles that he ought to attack, and he believed me, and gentle Dunois believed me, too. (*She faces front*) And so did La Hire and Xantrailles. They all believed me when I said we had to fight and . . .

PROMOTER (*moving above the fence down* R) Kill, Joan? And kill? And does Our Lord tell us to kill for what we want, as though we had fangs and claws?

(JOAN *does not reply*)

CAUCHON (*gently*) You loved the war, Joan.

("*Horse*" *music is heard*)

JOAN (*simply*) Yes. It is one of the sins for which I have most need of God's forgiveness. But in the evening I would look across the battlefield and cry because the joyful beginning to the morning had gone down in a heap of dead.

PROMOTER. And the next day, you began again?

JOAN. God wished it. While there remained one Englishman in France.

(*The* INQUISITOR *rises*)

It isn't difficult to understand. There was work to be done first, that was all. (*She turns to the others*) You are learned——

(*The others begin to exit*)

—and you think too much. You can't understand the simple things, but the dullest of my soldiers understands them.

(*The* PROMOTER *exits* RC)

Isn't that true, La Hire?

(LA HIRE, *in huge armour, gay and alarming, enters up* R *and stands* L *of the fence up* R.

CAUCHON *exits down* R. *The* INQUISITOR *exits over the rostrum down* L. WARWICK *exits up* R)

LA HIRE (*striding forward*) You bet it's true.

JOAN (*turning to face him*) La Hire . . .

LA HIRE (*taking up again the comradeship of the battle mornings*) Well, Miss, we've had the bit of praying, we agreed to have: what's the next thing? Do we take a bash at them this morning?

JOAN (*throwing herself into his arms*) It is my dear, fat La Hire. You smell so good.

LA HIRE (*taking an onion from his pouch; embarrassed*) An onion and a glass of wine. It's my usual morning meal. (*He leans on the fence* C) Excuse me, Miss: I know you don't like it, but I did my praying beforehand so that God shouldn't take against my breath.

(JOAN *jumps up and sits on the fence up* C)

Don't come too near: I know I stink in a way.

JOAN (*pressed against him*) No: it's good.

LA HIRE. You don't want to make me feel awkward. Usually you tell me I stink and it's a shame for a Christian. (*He crosses to the rostrum* LC, *sits on the second step, takes a map from his pouch and studies it*) Usually you say that if the wind carries in that direction I shall give us away to the English, I stink so much; and we shall ruin our ambush because of me. One quite small onion and two tots of red wine, no more. Of course, let's be honest, no water with it.

Joan. If I said that, I was a fool. If an onion has a right to stink why shouldn't you?

La Hire. It's what war does for you. Be a clerk, or a priest, or a linen draper: no smell. But be a captain, you're bound to sweat. As for washing, up in the line: a man doesn't see the interest in it. There was no need to add the onion, I suppose. (*He rises*) I ought to do with a bit of garlic sausage like the other fellows. But, look here, you wouldn't call it a sin, would you, eating the onion? (*He crosses to Joan*)

Joan (*smiling*) No, La Hire: not a sin.

La Hire. You never know with you, you know. (*He moves to the stool down C, sits and looks at his map*)

(*"Recorder" music is heard*)

Joan. Have I pestered you with sins, La Hire? I was silly to tease you so much: it's odd, but there you are, a great bear smelling of sweat and onions and wine, and think of nothing except the drinking and the fighting and the women.

La Hire (*looking up; very astonished*) Who, me? (*He puts his onion in his pouch*)

Joan. You. Yes. Look astonished, you old rogue. And yet you shine in the hand of God as bright as a new penny.

La Hire. Is that a fact? I should have thought I'd bitched my chance of paradise years ago. But do you think if I keep on praying a little bit every day as arranged, I might still get there?

Joan (*jumping from the fence, moving to L of La Hire and kneeling*) They're expecting you, La Hire. I know now God's paradise must be full of ruffians like you.

La Hire. Is that a fact? (*He rises*) It would make all the difference to feel there were a few kindred spirits about. I wasn't much enjoying the prospect of being in a crowd of saints and bishops looking like heaven's village idiot. (*He stands immediately in front of the stool*)

Joan. Great Jackass! (*She rises, stands on the stool and puts her arms around La Hire's neck*) Of course, heaven's full of dunces, hasn't Our Lord said so? It may even be they're the only ones who get there: the rest have so many brains to sin with they never get past the door.

La Hire. Is that a fact? You don't think, between ourselves, we'll get bored to death, do you, always on our best behaviour? Any fighting at all, do you imagine?

Joan. All the day long.

La Hire (*respectfully*) Wait now. Only when God isn't looking at us.

Joan (*taking the rolled map from him and hitting him over the head*)

But He's looking at you all the time, crackpot! He sees everything. And what's more, He's going to enjoy watching you at it.
"Go it, La Hire!" He'll say: "Bash the stuffing out of old Xantrailles. Pitch into him, now. Show him what you're made of!"

La Hire. Is that a fact?

Joan. Not in those words, perhaps, but in His own way.

La Hire (*enthusiastically*) By God, so He will!

Joan (*suddenly stern*) La Hire!

La Hire (*hanging his head*) Sorry, Miss. (*He moves* l)

Joan (*pitilessly*) If you swear He will throw you out.

La Hire (*moving to* l *of Joan*) I was feeling pleased, you see: I
had to thank Him somehow.

Joan. So He thought. But don't do it again. We've talked
quite enough for one morning. Let's get up on horseback and
take a look at the day.

(*"Horse" music is heard along with the clatter of hooves.* Joan *gets
off the stool. She and* La Hire *both mount imaginary horses and come
down* c, Joan r *of La Hire*)

La Hire. It's dead country this morning. Not a soul to see.

(*They are "riding" side by side*)

Joan. Look, we've got France all to ourselves—shall we ever
see the world to better advantage? Here on horseback side by side:
this is how it will be, La Hire, when the English have gone. Smell
the wet grass, La Hire; isn't this why men go fighting? To ride
out together smelling the world when the light of day is just
beginning to discover it.

La Hire. So anyone can who likes to take a walk in his garden.

Joan. No. I think death has to be somewhere near before God
will show us the world like this.

(*There is a pause. They penetrate into the country rocked by their
horses*)

La Hire. Suppose we should meet some English, who might
also be liking the good smells of the morning?

Joan. We attack them, we smite them, and send them flying.
That's what we're here for. (*She affects to rein in her horse*) Stop!

(*There is a short pause. They draw in their horses*)

(*She looks out front down* l) There are three English over there.
They've seen us. They're running away. No! Now they've turned
back again——

(La Hire *draws his sword*)

—they've seen there are only two of us. They're attacking. You're
not afraid, La Hire? No use counting on me; I'm only a girl, and
I've got no sword. Will you fight them alone?

("Horse" music is heard)

LA HIRE *(brandishing his sword; with a delighted roar)* Hell, yes, by God I will! *(He shouts towards the sky)* I didn't say anything, God, I didn't say anything. Pay no attention. *(He jumps up on to the top of the rostrum* LC) God, France and the Maid.

(LA HIRE *charges over the rostrum* L *and exits down* L)

JOAN *(running on to the top of the rostrum* LC) He didn't say anything, God. He didn't say anything. I will answer for him.

(A SOLDIER *enters down* R *and crosses to the bottom step of the rostrum* LC. *Another* SOLDIER *enters* RC, *crosses to the rostrum* LC, *and stands at the upstage side. The* SOLDIERS *grab Joan and throw her down* RC. *The* 1ST SOLDIER *exits* LC. *The* 2ND SOLDIER *exits* RC. *After a pause, Joan begins to speak, and the Court re-forms.*

The INQUISITOR *enters on the rostrum and sits on the top step* LC.
The PROMOTER *enters* RC *and stands behind the fence down* R.
CAUCHON *enters down* R.
WARWICK *enters* RC *and stands behind the fence up* R)

La Hire and Xantrailles! Oh, we're not at the end of things yet. They will come and deliver me with two or three or four hundred men.

CAUCHON *(quietly)* They came, Joan: right up to the gates of Rouen to find out how many of the English were in the town, and then they went away again.

JOAN *(dashed)* Oh, they went away? Without fighting? *(She pauses, recovers herself, rises and sits on the stool)* Why, they have gone to find reinforcements, of course. I myself taught them, it is no good to attack willynilly, as they did at Agincourt.

CAUCHON *(with a step towards Joan)* They withdrew to the south of the Loire; Charles is down there, disbanding his armies. He is tired of the war, and if he can he will make a treaty, to secure at least his own small portion of France. They will never come back again.

JOAN *(rising and moving to* L *of Cauchon)* It isn't true!

CAUCHON *(holding Joan's arms)* Joan. Have I ever lied to you, Joan? It is true. Then why will you sacrifice yourself to defend those who have deserted you? The only men on earth who are trying to save you—paradoxical though it may seem—are ourselves, your old enemies and now your judges. Recant, Joan: your resistance helps no-one now; your friends are betraying you. Return to the arms of your Mother Church.

(JOAN *crosses slowly to the stool down* R *and sits)*

Humble yourself, she will lift you up again. You needn't think of anything any more: you will do your penance, whether it be heavy or light, and at last you will be at peace. Surely you have a great need of peace.

JOAN (*after a pause*) In what concerns the Faith, I submit myself to the Church. (*She turns to the Inquisitor*) But what I have done I shall never wish to undo.

(CAUCHON *moves and stands below the fence up* C)

INQUISITOR (*rising*) Do you hear, my masters? Do you see Man raising up his head, like a serpent ready to strike us dead? Do you understand now what it is you have to judge? These heavenly Voices have deafened you as well as the girl, on my word they have. You have been labouring to discover what devil has been behind her actions. Would it were only a question of the devil. His trial would soon be over. The devil speaks our language. In his time he was an angel, and we understand him. The sum of his blasphemies, his insults, even his hatred of God, is an act of faith.

(CAUCHON *slowly turns and faces up stage.*)

But Man, calm and transparent as he seems, frightens me infinitely more. Look at him: in chains, disarmed, deserted, no longer sure even in himself—isn't that so, Joan—that the Voices which have been silent for so long have ever truly spoken. Does he throw himself down, supplicating God to hold him again in His hand? Does he at least implore his Voices to come back and give light to his path?

(JOAN *gazes out front*)

No. He turns away, suffers the torture, suffers humiliation and beating, suffers like a dumb animal, while his eyes fasten on the invincible image of himself—(*he thunders*) himself, his only true God. That is what I fear. And he replies—repeat it, Joan; you are longing to say it again: "But what I have done . . ."

JOAN (*quietly*) ". . . I shall never wish to undo."

INQUISITOR (*repeating*) "But what I have done I shall never wish to undo." You hear those words? And you will hear them said on the scaffold, at the stake, in the torture chamber, wherever they come to suffer for the errors they commit. And centuries hence they will be saying it; the hunting down of Man will go on endlessly. However powerful we become one day in one shape or another, however inexorably the Idea shall dominate the world, however rigorous, precise and subtle its organization and its police—(*he steps off the rostrum and crosses slowly towards Joan*) there will always be a man who has escaped, a man to hunt, who will presently be caught, presently be killed: a man who, even so, will humiliate the Idea at the highest point of its Power, simply because he will say "No" without lowering his eyes. (*He moves close to Joan, looks at her with hatred and hisses through his teeth*) An insolent breed! (*He moves up* RC *and stands between the Promoter and Cauchon*) Do you need to question her any more? Do you need to ask her why she threw herself from the height of the tower where she was imprisoned, whether to escape, or to destroy herself against the commandments of God? Why she has left her father and mother, put on the clothes of a man, and wears them still, against the commandments of the Church? She will give you the same reply—(*he crosses down* LC) the reply of Man: What I have done, I have done. It is mine, and my doing. No-one can take it from me; no-one can make me disown it. All that you can do is kill me, to make me cry out no matter what, under the torture, but make me say "Yes", you cannot do. (*He cries to them*) Ah well: by some means or other he must be taught to say "Yes", whatever it may cost the world. As long as one man remains who will not be broken, the Idea, even if it dominates and pervades all the rest of mankind, will be in danger of perishing. That is why I require Joan's excommunication, her rejection from the bosom of the Church and that she should be given over to the secular arm for punishment. (*He adds neutrally, reciting a formula*) Beseeching it nevertheless—beseeching it— to limit its sentence on this side of death and the mutilation of the limbs. (*He crosses himself, moves to the top of the rostrum* LC *and sits*) This will be a paltry victory against you, Joan, but at least it will silence you. And, up to now, we have not thought of a better.

CAUCHON (*gently*) My lord Inquisitor is the first to ask for your excommunication, Joan. In a moment I am afraid my lord Promoter will ask for the same thing. Each of us will speak his mind and then I shall have to give my decision. (*He claps his hands*)

(*The* HANGMAN *enters up* R *and crosses to* C. *The* PROMOTER *moves a little* R)

(*He indicates the Hangman*) Do you know this man, Joan?

(JOAN *turns to look at the Hangman and gives a little shudder of fear*)

It is the master hangman of Rouen. In a short while from now you will belong to him, unless you give your soul into our keeping so that we may save it. Is the stake ready, Master Hangman?

HANGMAN (*with his eyes fixed on Joan*) Quite ready, my lord. Higher than the regulation stake, such was the orders: so that the girl can be got a good view of from all sides. The nuisance of it for her, is that I shan't be able to help her at all, she will be too high up.

CAUCHON. What do you call helping her, Master Hangman?

HANGMAN. A trick of the trade, my lord: it's the custom, when there aren't any special instructions. You wait till the first flames get up, and then I climb up behind, under cover of the smoke, and strangle the party. Then it's only the corpse that burns, and it isn't so bad. But with the instructions I've had, it's too high, and I won't be able to get up there. (*Simply*) So, naturally, it will take longer. (*He steps back three paces*)

CAUCHON. Do you hear that, Joan?

JOAN (*softly*) Yes.

CAUCHON (*moving* RC) I am going to offer you once more the hand of your Mother, the great hand which opens towards you to take you back and save you. But the delay can't be for long. You hear the noise outside, as though the sea had come up to the door? That is the sound of the crowd, who already have been waiting for you since daybreak. They came early to get good places: and there they are still, eating the food they brought with them, grumbling at their children, laughing and joking, and asking the soldiers how long it will be before things begin to happen. (*He takes a step towards her*) They are not bad people. They are the same men and women who would have cheered you if you had captured Rouen. But things have turned out differently, that's all, and so instead they come to see you burned. As nothing very much ever happens to them, they make their adventures out of the triumphs or the deaths of the world's great ones. You will have to forgive them, Joan. All their lives long they pay dearly for being the common people; they deserve those little distractions.

JOAN (*quietly*) I do forgive them. And I forgive you, as well, my lord.

(CAUCHON *crosses to the rostrum* LC *and stands on the first step*)

PROMOTER (*speaking over the fence down* R) Appalling, abominable pride. My lord the Bishop troubles to talk to you like a father, in the hope of saving your miserable soul, and you have the effrontery to say that you forgive him.

JOAN (*rising and moving to the stool* C) My lord talks to me gently, but I don't know whether it is to save me or to overthrow me. And since in a little while he will have to burn me anyway, I forgive him. (*She sits on the stool*)

(*The* PROMOTER *moves and stands below the fence up* R)

CAUCHON (*moving to* L *of Joan*) Joan: try to understand that there is something absurd in your refusal. You are not an unbeliever. The God you claim as your own is ours also. And we are, in fact, those whom God has ordained to guide you, through the apostle Peter upon whom his Church is built. God did not say to His creatures: You will understand My will from Me. He said: "Thou and Peter, and upon this rock I will build My church—and its priests will be your shepherds . . ." Do you think us unworthy priests, Joan?

JOAN (*quietly*) No.

CAUCHON. Then why will you not do as God has said? Why

will you not resign your fault to the Church, as you did when you were a small girl, at home in your village? Has your faith so changed? (*He kneels* L *of Joan*)

JOAN (*crying out in anguish*) I want to submit to the Church. I want to receive the Holy Sacrament, but you won't let me.

CAUCHON. We will give it to you after your confession, and when your penance has begun; we only wait for you to say "Yes". You are brave, we know that indeed: but your flesh is still frail: you are surely afraid of dying?

JOAN (*quietly*) Yes. I am afraid. But what else can I do?

CAUCHON. Say to us: "I submit to you", say simply "Yes", and you will be at peace, blameless, and safe in your redemption.

JOAN (*suddenly exhausted*) Why will you torture me so gently, my lord? I would far rather you beat me.

CAUCHON (*smiling*) If I beat you, Joan, I should only add to your pride: your pride which wishes to see you persecuted and killed. I reason with you because God gifted you with reason and good sense. I beseech you, because I know you have gentle feeling. I am an old man, Joan; I have no more ambitions in this world, and, like each of us here, I have put many to death in defence of the Church, as you have put many to death in defence of your Voices. It is enough. I am tired. I wish to die without adding to those deaths the death of a little girl. Help me.

JOAN (*after a pause*) What do you want me to say?

(CAUCHON *rises, crosses above Joan and stands* L *of the fence down* R. JOAN *turns and faces Cauchon*)

CAUCHON. First of all you must understand that by insisting that God sent you, you no longer help anything or anyone. It is only playing into the hands of the English and the Executioner. Your King himself, has declared in his letters that he doesn't in any way wish to owe the possession of his crown to a divine intervention of which you were the instrument.

("*Cuckoo*" *music is heard.*
CHARLES *enters down* R *and stands behind the fence down* R. JOAN, *in distress, turns towards Charles*)

CHARLES. Put yourself in my place, Joan. If there had to be a miracle to crown me King of France, it means I wasn't naturally King at all. It means I wasn't the true son of my father, or else my coronation would have followed of its own accord. All the other Kings in my family have been crowned without needing a miracle. (*He crosses above Cauchon and stands up* L *of Joan*) Divine help is all very well in its way, but suspect. And it's even more suspect when it stops. Since that unhappy Paris business, we've been beaten at every step; and then you let yourself be captured at Compiegne. They've got a little verdict up their sleeve for you, to denounce you as a witch, a heretic, the devil's intermediary, all in one. I prefer people to think you were never sent by anyone, God or devil. (*He backs slowly towards the exit* LC) In that way, God has neither helped me, nor thrown me over. I won because I was the strongest at the time; I am being beaten now because I am the weakest, for the moment.

(CAUCHON *moves up* L *of Joan*)

That is healthy politics, if you understand?

(CHARLES *exits* LC)

JOAN (*softly*) Yes, I understand.

CAUCHON (*with a step towards Joan*) I'm thankful to see you're wiser at last. We have put so many questions to you, you became confused. I have to ask you three more, three essential ones. (*He moves to the rostrum* LC)

JOAN (*after a pause; quietly*) Ask them. I will see whether I can answer them.

CAUCHON (*sitting on the second step of the rostrum* LC) The first question is the really important one. If you answer "Yes", the other answers will take care of themselves. Listen carefully, weighing each word: Do you humbly ask to be received again into the bosom of the Church that she may estimate your deeds and judge you? It is enough for you to answer "Yes".

JOAN (*after a pause*) Yes, but . . .

INQUISITOR (*in a level voice*) With no "but".

JOAN. I do not wish to be made to deny what my Voices have said to me. I do not wish to be made to bear witness against my King, or to say anything which will dim the glory of his coronation which is his irrevocably now and for ever. (*She turns on her stool and faces up stage*)

INQUISITOR (*shrugging his shoulders*) Such is the voice of Man. There is only one way of bringing him to silence.

CAUCHON (*rising and crossing below Joan to* R *of her; becoming angry*) Joan, Joan, Joan, are you mad? Do you not see this man in red who is waiting for you? Realize—(*he moves above her*) understand, this is my last effort to save you; after this there is nothing more I can do. The Church still wishes to believe that you are one of her daughters. She has weighed with care the form her question should take, to help you on the path, and you cavil and try to bargain. There is no bargaining with your Mother, you impudent girl! You should beg her on your knees to wrap—— (*he moves* L *of Joan*)

(JOAN *falls to her knees* L *of the stool and faces front*)

—you in her cloak of love and protect you. The penance which she will inflict on you, you will offer up to God, with the injustice of it, if you find injustice there. Our Lord suffered far more than you in the humiliation and injustice of His Passion. Did He bargain or cavil when He came to die for you? Your suffering bears no comparison with His: scourged, mocked, spat upon: crowned with thorns, and nailed in a long agony between two thieves——

(JOAN *gives a cry*)

—you can never hope to rival His suffering. (*He kneels* L *of Joan*) And He asks, through us, only one thing of you, that you submit to the judgement of His Church, and you hesitate.

JOAN (*after a pause; tears in her eyes*) Forgive me, my lord. I hadn't thought that Our Saviour might wish it. He has surely suffered more than I. (*She pauses*) I submit.

CAUCHON. Do you humbly and without any restriction supplicate the Holy Catholic Church to receive you again into her bosom, and do you defer to her judgement?

JOAN. I humbly supplicate my Mother Church to receive me again into her bosom and I surrender myself to her judgement.

CAUCHON (*patting Joan's head, with a sigh of relief*) Good, Joan; well done. The rest will be simple enough now. (*He rises, moves to the rostrum* LC *and sits on the second step*) Do you promise never again to take up arms?

JOAN (*heavily*) Yes.

CAUCHON. Do you promise never to wear again these man's clothes, which is contrary to all the rules of decency and Christian modesty?

JOAN (*tired of the question*) The clothes are nothing. My Voices told me to wear them.

PROMOTER (*crossing to* R *of the rostrum* LC) Will you note that, my lord? She treats her indecency as something to glory in, boasts of it, in fact, takes a gross delight in it, I've no doubt. If she submits to the Church, as she apparently wants to, I may have to give up my chief accusation of heresy; but as long as she refuses to put off this diabolical dress, I shall persist in my charge of witchcraft, even though pressure is put upon me by the conspiracy to shield her which I see presides over this debate. I shall appeal if necessary to the Council of Basle. The devil is in this, my lord. (*He crosses to the fence down* R) The devil is in it. I can feel his terrible presence. (*He moves down* RC) He it is who is making her refuse to give up these clothes of immodesty and vice, no doubt of that. (*He crosses himself*)

JOAN. Put me in a Church prison, and I won't refuse them.

PROMOTER (*moving to* R *of Joan*) You snall not make your bargains with the Church: my lord has already told you so. You will give up this dress altogether, or you will be condemned as a witch and burnt.

CAUCHON. Why don't you wish to obey us now, in the prison where you are?

JOAN. I am not alone there.

PROMOTER. Well? You're not alone there. Well? What of that?

JOAN (*rising and sitting on the stool* C) English soldiers are on guard in the cell, all through the day, and through the night.

PROMOTER. Well? (*He pauses*) Do you mean to go on? Your powers of invention have failed you already, is that it? I should have thought the devil was more ingenious. You feel that you've been caught out, my girl, and it makes you blush.

CAUCHON (*quietly*) You must answer him, Joan. I think I understand, but it must be you who tells us so.

JOAN (*after a moment of hesitation*) The nights are long, my lord. I am in chains. I do my best to keep awake, but sleep sometimes is too strong for me. (*She stops*)

PROMOTER (*crossing below Joan to* L *of her; more and more obtuse*) Well, what then? The nights are long, you are in chains, you want to sleep. What then?

JOAN (*quietly*) I can defend myself better if I wear these clothes.

(*There is a pause. The* PROMOTER *moves up and stands behind the fence* C)

CAUCHON (*heavily*) Has this been so all the time of the trial?

JOAN. Ever since I was captured, my lord, and each night, and when you send me back there, it begins again. I've got into the way of not sleeping now, which is why my answers are muddled when I'm brought before you in the mornings.

CAUCHON. Why don't you call the officer, and he would defend you?

JOAN (*after a pause*) They told me they would be hanged if I called for help.

WARWICK (*moving down* RC; *to Cauchon*) Incredible! I never heard of such a thing. Quite possible in the French army. But in the English army, no, quite ridiculous. I shall inquire into this.

(WARWICK *exits up* R)

CAUCHON (*rising and moving to* L *of Joan*) If you would return, Joan, back to your Mother, the Church who is waiting for you: promise to change from these clothes to the dress of a girl: the Church, from now on, would see you had no such fears.

JOAN. Then I do promise.

CAUCHON (*giving a deep sigh*) Good. Thank you, Joan, you have helped me. I was afraid for a time we should have no power to save you. We shall read your promise to adjure your sins: the document is all ready, you have only to sign it (*He moves to the rostrum* LC)

JOAN. I don't know how to write. (*She rises*)

(*The* PROMOTER *moves and stands above the rostrum* LC)

CAUCHON (*turning to Joan*) You will make a cross. (*To the*

Inquisitor) My lord Inquisitor, allow me to recall Brother
Ladvenu so that he may read this to the prisoner.

(JOAN *crosses slowly to the stool down* R *and sits*)

It is Brother Ladvenu who is responsible, at my request, for
drawing up this paper. And, moreover, we have all to be here
now, to pronounce sentence, now that Joan has returned to us.
(*He leans towards him*) You should be gratified, my lord: Man
has said "Yes". (*He crosses to the entrance* RC)

INQUISITOR (*a pallid smile on his thin lips*) I am waiting until the
conclusion; until the conclusion.

CAUCHON (*calling*) Brother Ladvenu!

PROMOTER (*leaning over the rostrum and whispering*) My lord
Inquisitor, you won't allow them to do this?

INQUISITOR (*with a vague gesture*) If she has said "Yes" . . .

(CAUCHON *moves* C)

PROMOTER. My lord Bishop has conducted the enquiry with an
indulgence towards the girl which I can't begin to understand.
And yet I have reliable information that he feeds well from the
English manger. Does he feed even more rapaciously from the
French? That is what I ask myself.

(LADVENU *enters* RC. *The* PROMOTER *moves up* L.
 WARWICK *enters up* R *and stands behind the fence up* C.
 A SOLDIER *enters down* R. *He carries a small writing-desk with
an inkwell, quill and sand sifter. He fits the desk on the top of the fence
down* R, *then exits down* R)

CAUCHON (*to Ladvenu*) She is saved, Brother Ladvenu, Joan is
saved. She has agreed to return to us, and to Holy Mother
Church. Read her the Act of Abjuration, and she will sign it.
(*He crosses to the rostrum* LC *and sits on the second step*)

(JOAN *rises and steps a little up stage*)

LADVENU (*moving down* RC) Thank you, Joan. (*He produces a
large scroll, the Act of Abjuration*) I was praying for you: I prayed
that this might be possible. (*He reads from the scroll*) "I, Joan,
known as the Maid, confess to having sinned, by pride, obstinacy,
and wrong-doing, in pretending to receive revelation from Our
Lord God, Father of all Men. I confess to having blasphemed by
wearing immodest clothing, and to having, by my persuasion,
incited men to kill one another. I forswear and abjure all these
sins; I vow upon the Holy Gospels no more to wear these clothes
or to bear arms. I promise to surrender myself in humility to our
Holy Mother Church, and I declare myself ready to suffer the
sentence which it will please her to inflict upon me. In token of
which I have signed my name to this Act of Abjuration which I

profess I have understood." (*He motions to Joan and turns to the desk*)

JOAN (*moving to R of Ladvenu; seeming now like a shy and awkward girl*) Do I make a circle or a cross? I can't write my name.

LADVENU. I will guide your hand.

(LADVENU *helps* JOAN *to sign, then turns to Cauchon.* JOAN *faces up stage*)

CAUCHON. There; it is done, Joan; and the Church rejoices to see her daughter safely returned. Your soul is saved, and your body will not be delivered up to the executioner. (*He rises*)

(*The* INQUISITOR *rises.* LADVENU *passes* JOAN *to* C)

We condemn you only, through the mercy and the grace of God, to live the rest of your days a prisoner, in penitence of these errors, eating the bread of sorrow, drinking the water of anguish, so that in solitary contemplation you may repent; and by these means we shall admit you free of the danger of excommunication into which you were fallen.

(JOAN *looks at* LADVENU, *who looks away*)

You may go in peace. (*He makes the sign of the cross over her*) Take her away.

(JOAN *looks at Cauchon.*

LADVENU *leads* JOAN *up* C *and they exit up* L. *The* PROMOTER *exits* LC. *The* INQUISITOR *exits over the rostrum down* L. CAUCHON *crosses to the fence down* R.

Two SOLDIERS *enter down* R. *The* 1ST SOLDIER *removes the desk and exits with it down* R. *The* 2ND SOLDIER *moves the stool down* C *and places it down* RC, *then exits down* R)

WARWICK (*moving down* LC) Good enough, my lord; good enough. I was wondering for a moment or so what irresponsible whim was urging you to save the girl, and whether you hadn't a slight inclination to betray your King.

CAUCHON. Which king, my lord?

WARWICK (*crossing to* L *of Cauchon; with a touch of frigidity*) I said your King. I imagine you have only one? Yes; very uncertain for a time whether His Majesty was going to get his money's worth, owing to this fancy of yours. But then, when I thought about it, I could see. The resolute, unshakable girl, tied to the stake and burning in the flames, would have seemed, even so, something of a triumph for the French cause. This admission of guilt, on the other hand, is properly disgraceful. Perfect.

(WARWICK *exits* RC.

CAUCHON *exits down* R.

The HANGMAN *exits* LC. *Two strokes of the prison bell are heard, followed by "Cuckoo" music.*

A Soldier *enters* RC *and places the fence up* R *alongside but behind the fence down* R. *The* 2ND Soldier *enters* LC, *picks up the fence* C *and stands it on end, diagonally up and down stage* C. *He then stands up* C. *The* 1ST Soldier *exits. See Ground Plan E.*

Joan *enters* LC *and crosses slowly to* C.

Agnes *and* Yolande *enter up* R. *They are followed by the* Queen. Charles *enters* LC)

Agnes (*moving to* R *of Joan*) Joan, Joan, my dear; we're so very happy it has all turned out well for you. Congratulations!

Yolande (*moving up* L *of Joan*) Dying is quite useless, my little Joan: and whatever we do in life should have a use of some kind.

(Joan *does not look at them. She hears their prattle without seeming to hear it*)

Agnes. It was all so very stupid. Usually I adore political trials, and I particularly begged Charles to get me a seat; to watch someone fighting for his life is desperately exciting, as a rule. But really I didn't feel in the least happy when I was there. All the time I kept saying to myself: This is so very stupid——

(Yolande *moves above the rostrxms* LC. *The* Queen *stands up* C)

—this poor little tomboy, she is going to get herself killed, and all for nothing. Being alive is much better, you know, in every way.

Charles (*moving behind the fence* C) Yes, of course it is; and when you practically ruined your chances, just because of me— well, I was very touched, naturally, but I didn't know how to make you understand that you were getting everything quite wrong.

(Joan *moves down* C. Agnes *moves to* R *of Joan*)

In the first place, as you might expect, I had taken the precaution to disown you, on the advice of that old fox of an Archbishop; but, more than that, I don't like people being devoted to me. I don't like being loved. It creates obligations, and obligations are detestable.

(*The* Soldier *moves to the fences down* R. *The* 1ST Soldier *enters down* R. *The two* Soldiers *stand the two fences on end and place them* RC, *triangle shape, forming a cell. They then exit. See Ground Plan F*)

Joan (*to Agnes; suddenly and quietly*) Take care of Charles. I hope he keeps his courage.

Agnes. Of course he will; why shouldn't he? My way with him is not so different from yours. I don't want him to be a poor little King who is always being beaten, any more than you do; and you shall see, I shall make our Charles a great King yet, and without getting myself burnt, either. (*In a low voice*) I suppose it may be rather disillusioning to say so, Joan—though, of course, the two sexes are presumably what God wanted—but I do seem to get as much out of Charles by my little campaigns in the bedroom as ever you did with swords and angels.

JOAN (*murmuring*) Poor Charles. (*She crosses to the stool down* RC *and sits, facing up stage*)

(AGNES *goes round to the back of the cell, stands* R *of it and looks through the bars made by the fences*)

AGNES. Why poor? He is perfectly happy, like all egoists: and one of these days he is going to be a great king into the bargain.

YOLANDE. We shall see that done, Joan: not your way, but ours, and effectively enough.

AGNES (*with a gesture to the Queen*) Even her little Majesty will help.

(*The* QUEEN *crosses to the left side of the cell and looks through the bars*)

She has just given him a second son. It is all she can do, but she does it very well. So if the first son dies there is no feverish worry. The succession is assured. You can be quite happy, Joan, that you're leaving everything in good order at the Court of France.

(*"Cuckoo" music is heard*)

CHARLES (*after a sneeze*) Are you coming, my dear?

(*The* QUEEN *moves up* C. YOLANDE *crosses to the exit* LC)

This prison atmosphere is deadly, so damp it would really be healthier to sit in the river. Good-bye, Joan, for the moment; we'll come and visit you from time to time.

(*The* QUEEN *moves up* LC. AGNES *moves up* RC)

JOAN. Good-bye, Charles.

CHARLES (*moving up* L) Good-bye, good-bye. I might say— (*he turns and comes back to the fence* C) if ever you come back to Court, you will have to call me Sire, like anybody else. I've seen to that, since my coronation. Even La Tremouille does it. It's a great victory.

(CHARLES *exits up* L. *The* QUEEN *follows him off.*
YOLANDE *exits* LC. AGNES *exits up* R. JOAN *rises and faces up stage, looking through the bars*)

JOAN (*murmuring*) Good-bye, Sire. I am glad I got you that privilege at least. (*She kneels behind the stool, facing front*) Blessed St Michael, blessed ladies Catherine and Margaret, are you never going to come again and speak to me? Why have you left me alone since the English captured me? You were there to see me

safely to victory: but it's now, in the suffering time, that I need
you most. I know it would be too simple, too easy, if God always
held me by the hand: I know He took my hand at the beginning
because I was still too small to be alone, and later He thought I
could make my own way. But I still need help, God. (*She rises and
sits on the stool*) It was very difficult to follow clearly everything
the Bishop said to me. He spoke so gently, and it often seemed
that he was right. Are you sure that you meant that, God? Did
you mean me to be so afraid of suffering? Are you sure that you
want me to live? (*She pauses. She seems to be waiting for an answer,
her eyes on the sky*) No word for me? I shall have to answer that
question for myself as well. (*She pauses, then nods*) Perhaps after all
I am proud and self-willed; perhaps after all I did imagine
everything.

(WARWICK, *preceded by a* SOLDIER, *enters over the rostrum down* L.
JOAN *suddenly bursts into tears.* WARWICK *stops on the top step of the
rostrum and looks at Joan, surprised.*
      The SOLDIER *exits over the rostrum*)

WARWICK. Are you crying?
JOAN. Yes, my lord.
WARWICK. But I came here to congratulate you. That was a
very happy solution to it all, I thought, the outcome of the trial,
very. (*He crosses to* L *of Joan*) I told Cauchon, I was delighted
you managed to avoid an execution. Quite apart from my own
personal sympathy for you, the suffering is really frightful, you
know, and quite useless, and most unpleasant to watch. I'm
perfectly convinced you've done right to steer clear of martyrdom;
better for us all. I congratulate you most sincerely. It was
astonishing, considering the peasant stock you come from, that
you should behave with such distinction. (*He crosses behind the
fences to* R *of Joan*) A gentleman is always ready, when he must,
to die for his honour or his king, but the *hoi polloi* will get themselves killed for nothing. And then I was very entertained to see
you queen the Inquisitor's pawn. (*He moves up* R *of Joan*) A
sinister character, that Inquisitor fellow. I detest intellectuals
more than anybody. These fleshless people, what unpleasant
fossils they are. (*He runs a finger along a bar of the cell, then crosses to
L of Joan*) Are you really a virgin?
JOAN. Yes.
WARWICK. Well, yes, of course you are. No woman would have
spoken quite in the way you did. (*He crosses to* C) My fiancée in
England, who's a very innocent girl, reasons exactly like a boy
herself, and, like you, there's no gainsaying her. There's an
Indian proverb—I don't know whether you may have heard it—
which says it takes a virgin to walk on water. (*He gives a little
laugh and moves to* L *of Joan*) We shall see how long she manages
that, once she becomes Lady Warwick. Being a virgin is a state

of grace. We adore them, and revere them, and yet, the sad thing is, as soon as we meet one we're in the greatest possible hurry to make a woman of her: and we expect the miracle to go on as if nothing had happened. (*He crosses to* c)   Madmen! Just as soon as ever this campaign is over—it won't be long now, I hope: your little Charles is tottering to a fall—but as soon as it is, back I go to England, to do that very same idiotic thing. (*He gazes out front*)   Warwick Castle is a very beautiful place, a bit big, a bit severe, but very beautiful. I breed horses—and my fiancée rides rather well, not as well as you do, but rather well. So she ought to be very happy there. We shall go fox-hunting, of course, and entertain fairly lavishly from time to time. I'm only sorry the circumstances make it so difficult to invite you over. (*He pauses awkwardly, then takes a step towards Joan*)   Well, there it is, I thought I'd pay you this visit, rather like shaking hands after a match, if you know what I mean. I hope I haven't disturbed you. (*He crosses to* LC *and turns*)   Are my men·behaving themselves now?

JOAN. Yes.

WARWICK. I should think they will certainly transfer you to a Church prison. But in any case, until they do, if there's any sign of a lapse, don't hesitate to report it to me. I'll have the black-guard hanged. It's not really possible to have a whole army of gentlemen, but we can try. (*He goes on to the first step of the rostrum and bows*)   Madam. (*He turns to go*)

JOAN (*calling*)   My lord!

WARWICK (*stopping and turning*)   Yes?

JOAN (*without looking at him*)   It would have been better, wouldn't it, if I had been burned?

WARWICK. I told you, for His Majesty's Government, the admission of guilt was just as good.

JOAN. But for me?

WARWICK. Unprofitable suffering. An ugly business. (*He crosses to* c)   No, really, it wouldn't have been better. It would have been, as I told you just now, slightly plebeian, and ill-bred, and more than slightly stupid, to insist on dying just to embarrass everybody and make a demonstration.

JOAN (*rising and moving to Warwick; as though to herself*)   But I am ill-bred, I am stupid. And then, remember, my lord, my life isn't prepared and perfected like yours, running so smoothly between war, hunting, and your beautiful bride waiting for you in England. What is left of me when I am not Joan any longer?

WARWICK. Life isn't going to be very gay for you, I agree, not at first, anyway. But things will adjust themselves in time, I don't think you need have any doubt of that.

JOAN (*crossing below Warwick to the rostrum* LC)   Do you see what I shall be like when things have adjusted themselves: set free, perhaps, and vegetating at the French Court on a small pension?

WARWICK (*moving to* R *of Joan; impatiently*) My dear girl, I can tell you, in six months there won't be a French Court.

JOAN (*sitting on the downstage corner of the rostrum; almost laughing, though sadly*) Accepting everything, fat and complacent. Can you see me painted and powdered, trying to look fashionable? Who knows, perhaps even with a husband.

WARWICK. Why not? Everything has to come to an end sometime. I'm going to be married myself.

JOAN (*rising and suddenly crying out in another voice*) But I don't want everything to come to an end. Or at least not an end like that—(*she crosses below Warwick to* C) an end which is no end at all. (*She kneels down* C, *facing front*) Blessed St Michael: St Margaret: St Catherine. You may be silent now, but I wasn't born until you first spoke to me, that day in the fields: my life truly began when I did what you told me to do, and you kept yourself silent, God, while all the priests were seeking to speak at once, and everything became a confusion of words. But you told St Michael to make it clear to me in the very beginning, that when you're silent you have then the most certain trust in us. It is the time when you let us take on everything alone. (*She rises and draws herself up*) Well, I take it on, O God: I take it upon myself. I give Joan back to you: true to what she is, now and forever. (*She backs into the cell*) Call your soldiers, Warwick——

(WARWICK *steps down* LC *and faces Joan*)

—call them, call them, quickly now: for I tell you I withdraw my admission of guilt: I take back my promises: they can pile their faggots, and set up their stake: they can have their holiday after all. (*She runs on to the top of the rostrum* LC *and calls*) Hey, there, soldiers!

WARWICK (*turning to face Joan*) Now, for God's sake don't let's have any such nonsense, I do implore you. I told you, I'm very satisfied with things as they are. And besides, I loathe executions. I couldn't bear to watch you being burned.

JOAN. You have to have courage, that's all; I shall have courage. (*She moves down to the first step of the rostrum, looks at Warwick's pale face and puts a hand on his shoulder*) You're a good, dear fellow, in spite of your gentlemanly poker-face; but there isn't anything you can do; we belong, as you say, to different ways of life. (*She unexpectedly gives him a little kiss on the cheeks, runs into the cell and calls*) Soldiers! Hey there, soldiers. Fetch me the clothes I wore to fight in——

(*Two* SOLDIERS *enter down* R)

—(*she knocks down the two fences down* R) and when I'm back——

(*The two* SOLDIERS *catch the fences and exit with them down* R.
The 3RD SOLDIER *enters up* L)

—in my breeches—— (*she knocks down the fence* C)

(*The* 3RD SOLDIER *catches the fence* C *and exits with it up* L)

—tell all my judges Joan is herself again.

(JOAN *exits up* R. WARWICK *remains alone, wiping his cheek*)

WARWICK. How out of place this all is. What bad form. It's impossible to get on well with these French for long.

(WARWICK *exits* LC. *A great clamour is heard off, and the crowd are heard shouting "To the stake with the witch."*
    The PROMOTER *enters* LC)

PROMOTER (*moving down* C; *yelling*)   To the stake with the witch. To the stake.

(*Two* SOLDIERS *enter down* L *and carry the rostrums to* C)

Shave her head, the soldiers' bitch! To the stake! To the stake! (*He jumps on to the rostrum as it is placed* C)   Burn her! *Burn her!*

(*The* SOLDIERS *exit* LC. *The crowd off now take up a steady chant, "Burn her."*
    WARWICK *enters* LC, *moves to the Promoter and pulls him off the rostrum*)

WARWICK. Stupidity! Absurd stupidity! This is something we could have done without, perfectly well.

(*A* SOLDIER *and the* HANGMAN *bring on the stake* LC *and place it over the rostrum* C.
    The PROMOTER *exits down* R. *The* HANGMAN *gets on to the rostrum and stands by the stake.*
    JOAN *is dragged on* RC *by two* SOLDIERS. *They take her to the stake, where the* HANGMAN *receives her and chains her to the stake*)

JOAN (*as she is brought on*)   A cross! Let me have a cross to hold: pity me.

(*A* SOLDIER *exits* RC *and another* SOLDIER *exits* LC.
    The PROMOTER *enters down* R *with a fence, which he stands in front of the stake*)

PROMOTER (*leaning on the fence*)   No, no! No cross for a witch.

(CAUCHON *enters up* R *and stands above the stake.*
    LADVENU *enters up* R *and crosses to* LC)

JOAN. Give me a cross, a crucifix.
CAUCHON (*moving down* R *of the stake*)   Ladvenu!

(LADVENU *moves down* C)

To the parish church. Run, Ladvenu!

(LADVENU *runs off* LC.
    The INQUISITOR *enters down* L)

PROMOTER (*to the Inquisitor*) A cross. This is most irregular. Aren't you going to protest, my lord?

(*The two* SOLDIERS *enter* LC *and* RC, *carrying the two remaining fences. They place them leaning against each side of the stake, so as to form a pyramid. See Ground Plan G.*
An ENGLISH SOLDIER *enters up* R *and stands behind the stake*)

INQUISITOR (*staring at Joan*) With or without a crucifix, she has to be silenced, and quickly. Look at her defying us.

(MOTHER, FATHER *and* BROTHER *enter down* R, *cross and stand up* L)

JOAN. A cross!

(*The* ENGLISH SOLDIER *standing behind the stake, has taken two sticks and tied them together*)

ENGLISH SOLDIER. Hold on a bit, here you are. (*He climbs on to the stake and hands the improvised cross to Joan*) She's a right to a cross like anybody else.
PROMOTER. She is a heretic. I forbid you to give it to her.
ENGLISH SOLDIER. You . . . (*He climbs down*)

(JOAN *kisses the cross. The* HANGMAN *forces Joan's hands behind her and continues chaining her*)

PROMOTER (*rushing to Warwick*) My lord! This man ought to be arrested as a heretic. I insist that you arrest him immediately.

(*The three* SOLDIERS *meet* LC)

WARWICK. You make me tired, sir. I have eight hundred men like that, each one more heretical than the others. They are what I use to fight the wars with. (*He moves down* R)

(LADVENU *enters* LC, *carrying a cross. The* PROMOTER *moves* C)

INQUISITOR (*to the Hangman*) Will you hurry and light the fire? Let the smoke cover her quickly, and hide her away out of our sight.

(*The three* SOLDIERS *move hurriedly up* C. *The* HANGMAN *moves* L *of the stake. The rest of the cast enter up* R *and up* L. CHARLES *stands* L *of the stake.* YOLANDE, AGNES *and the* QUEEN *stand* RC. LA HIRE *and the* PAGE *stand up* RC. BEAUDRICOURT *stands up* RC. *The* 1ST SOLDIER *moves down* R, *and the* 2ND SOLDIER *moves up* R. *The* 3RD SOLDIER *moves up* L)

We must be quick. We must be quick! We must be quick!
HANGMAN (*throwing an imaginary lighted faggot*) There!

(*The* CROWD *give a gasp of horror, kneel and commence to pray.* LADVENU *climbs up to* L *of Joan, holding his cross*)

LADVENU. Courage, Joan. We are all praying for you.

(*The "De Profundis" is heard*)

JOAN. Thank you, little brother. But get down: the flames will catch you: you will be burnt as well.

(LADVENU *climbs down and stands up* R *of the Inquisitor, holding his cross towards Joan*)

INQUISITOR (*to the Hangman, unable to bear it any more*) Well, man, have you done it yet, have you done it?
HANGMAN. Yes, it's done, my lord, it's alight. In two minutes the flames will have reached her. (*He moves up* C)
INQUISITOR (*kneeling down* L; *with a sigh of relief*) At last!
CAUCHON (*falling on his knees*) Oh God, forgive us.

(*They all kneel, and start the prayers for the dead. The* PROMOTER, *in a fury of hatred, remains standing*)

Down on your knees, Canon. Get down on your knees.

(*The* PROMOTER, *looking like a cornered animal, kneels* LC)

INQUISITOR (*who dare not look; to Ladvenu*) Is she looking straight in front of her?
LADVENU. Yes, my lord.
INQUISITOR. Without flinching?
LADVENU. Yes, my lord.
INQUISITOR (*almost sorrowfully*) And there is almost a smile on her lips, is there not?
LADVENU. Yes, my lord.
INQUISITOR (*with bowed head, overwhelmed; heavily*) I shall never be able to master him.
LADVENU (*radiant with confidence and joy*) No, my lord.

(*The* HANGMAN *throws fuel on to the fire. The* CROWD *draw away*)

JOAN (*already twisted with pain; murmuring*) Blessed Michael, Margaret, and Catherine, you were brighter than these flames: let your voices burn me. O Lord Jesus, let them speak to me. Speak to me. In the fields, in the heat of the sun. Noon.

(*The prayers are louder*)

BEAUDRICOURT (*after a pause; rising*) Stop! Stop! Wait now. This can't be the way it goes. (*He moves down* LC)

(LADVENU *moves* C)

Grant a stay of execution—we haven't done what we said we'd do. We haven't performed a coronation.

(WARWICK *rises*)

We said that we were going to play everything. And we haven't
at all. It isn't justice to her, she has the right to see the coronation performed; it's part of her story.
CAUCHON. We did say so, indeed. (*He rises*)

(*The* INQUISITOR *rises*)

You were right to remind us. (*He crosses to* LC) You remember,
gentlemen: the whole of her life to go through was what we said.

(CHARLES *rises*)

We were in too great a hurry to bring her to an end. We were
committing an injustice.

(LA HIRE *and the* PAGE *rise*)

CHARLES (*moving to* R *of Cauchon*) You see! I knew they would
forget my coronation. No-one ever remembers my coronation.
And look what it cost me.

(*The remainder of the* CROWD *slowly rise.*
   The PAGE *exits* RC)

WARWICK. Well, really! The coronation, now. As though their
little victory came last. It would be most improper for me to
attend any such ceremony; I shall go away. As far as I am concerned it is all over, and Joan is burnt. His Majesty's Government
has obtained its political objective.

(WARWICK *exits down* R)

CAUCHON. Unchain her.

(*The* HANGMAN *goes on to the stake and unchains Joan*)

Drag away the faggots.

(*The* PROMOTER *exits* R
   The INQUISITOR *takes the cross from Ladvenu and exits down* L)

Give her the sword and the banner again. This man is quite
right——

(*Organ music is heard*)

—the real end of Joan's story—(*he faces front*) the end which will
never come to an end——

(BEAUDRICOURT *moves up* L)

—which they will always tell, long after they have forgotten our
names or confused them all together: it isn't the painful and
miserable end of the cornered animal caught at Rouen: but the
lark——

(*The three* SOLDIERS *move the fences away from the stake.*
     The PAGE *enters down* R *with* *Joan's banner.* JOAN *climbs
down from the stake, takes the banner and stands* RC)

—singing in the open sky.

(*The* PAGE *exits down* R)

Joan at Rheims in all her glory. The true end of the story is a
kind of joy. Joan of Arc: a story which ends happily.

The HANGMAN *clears the chains from the stake.* LA HIRE,
FATHER, BROTHER *and the* HANGMAN *each take a corner of the
rostrum containing the stake complete, and move the whole unit up stage
and place it across the corner of the set up* LC. BROTHER *climbs on to
the rostrum and makes the stake into a cross by turning a cross beam
from behind the stake, the whole thing forming into an altar. As they
do this, the three* SOLDIERS *place the fences round the altar, leaving a
gap in front of it, forming the altar rail. A picture is formed. The*
HANGMAN *and the* ENGLISH SOLDIER *exit up* L. CAUCHON *and*
LADVENU *kneel down* RC. *The* PAGE *enters down* R, *with a crown
on a cushion. He crosses to the altar and stands below it. He is followed
by the* ARCHBISHOP, *who crosses and stands on the first step of the
altar.* CHARLES *moves to the altar and kneels in front of the* ARCH-
BISHOP. YOLANDE, AGNES *and the* QUEEN *kneel* R. FATHER,
MOTHER *and* BROTHER *kneel up* RC. *The* SOLDIERS *move up* C *and
kneel.* LA HIRE *and* BEAUDRICOURT *move down* L *and kneel.* JOAN
stands up C, *holding her banner. The sound of the* Te Deum *swells. The*
ARCHBISHOP *takes the crown and holds it high. He lowers the crown to
Charles' head as—*

                    the CURTAIN *falls*

MADE AND PRINTED IN GREAT BRITAIN BY
LATIMER TREND & COMPANY LTD PLYMOUTH

FURNITURE AND PROPERTY LIST

PART I

On stage—3 rostrums LC (*unpinned*)
      Fence C
      Fence down R
      Fence up R
      Stool down C
      Stool down R
      Stick for FATHER against wall down R

Off stage—Book (PROMOTER)
      Pair of trestles (SOLDIER)
      Tray. *On it:* wine jug, tankard, bowl of fruit, plate (SOLDIER)
      Throne chair. *In seat box:* playing cards (prepared), several scrolls,
               plain sheet of parchment, quill pen, inkstand
               On it: 2 black cushions (SOLDIERS)
      3 embroidery frames with needles, wools, etc. (YOLANDE, AGNES,
          QUEEN)

Personal—WARWICK: gloves, stick
      MOTHER: knitting
      FATHER: belt
      BEAUDRICOURT: knife
      CHARLES: cup-and-ball, book
      ARCHBISHOP: eyeglass, ring
      CAUCHON: ring

PART II

Setting as at the beginning of Part I
(*The rostrums LC are pin-hinged together*)

Off stage—Writing desk to fit on fence. *On it:* inkwell, quill, sand sifter (SOLDIER)
      Cross on pole (LADVENU)
      Stake with three chains attached (HANGMAN and SOLDIER)
      Two small sticks and cord for making cross (ENGLISH SOLDIER)
      Joan's banner (PAGE)
      Crown on cushion (PAGE)

Personal—LA HIRE: map, onion casing with apple inside, sword
      LADVENU: large scroll (Act of Abjuration)

LIGHTING PLOT

EFFECTS PLOT

PART I

THE LARK

Cue 18 LADVENU: ". . . praying for you." (page 66)
"De Profundis" is heard until BEAUDRICOURT *cries "Stop!"*

Cue 19 CAUCHON: ". . . man is quite right." (page 67)
"Organ" music is heard
Fade after "Te Deum" starts

Cue 20 CAUCHON: ". . . but the lark . . ." (page 67)
The "Te Deum" is heard
This continues until the CURTAIN *falls*

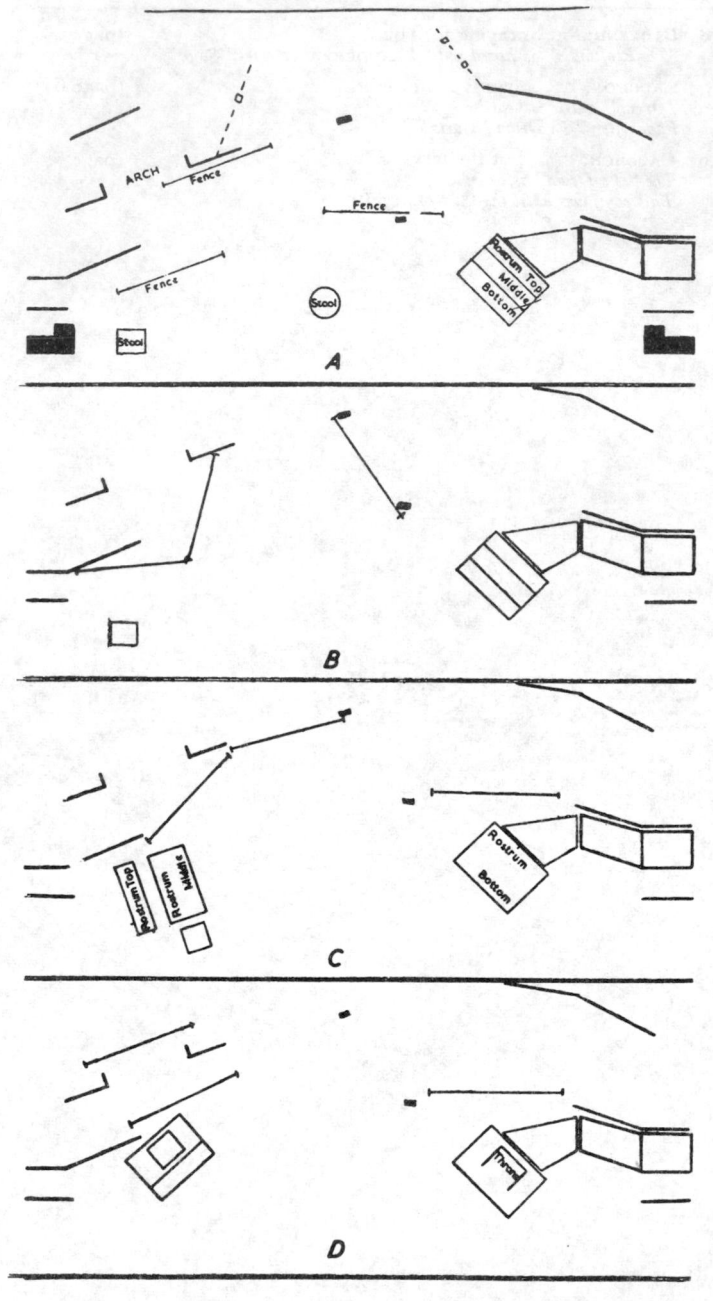

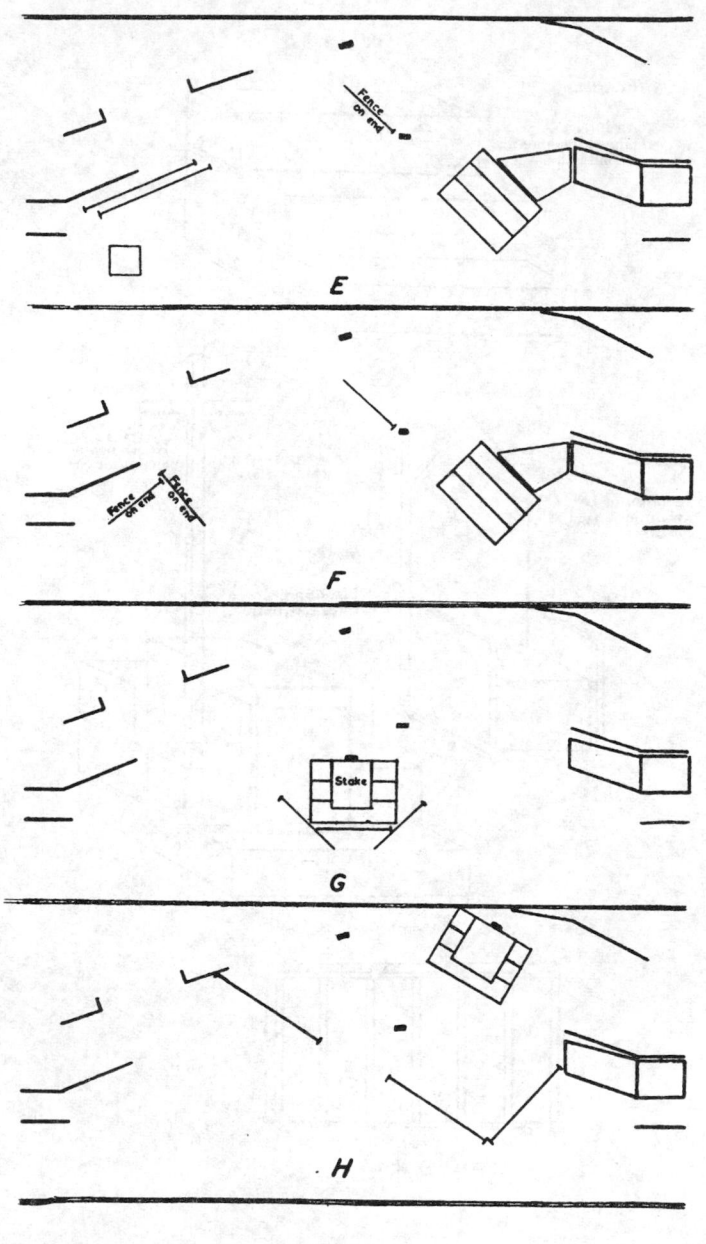

E

Fence on end

F

Fence on end   Fence on end

G

Stake

H

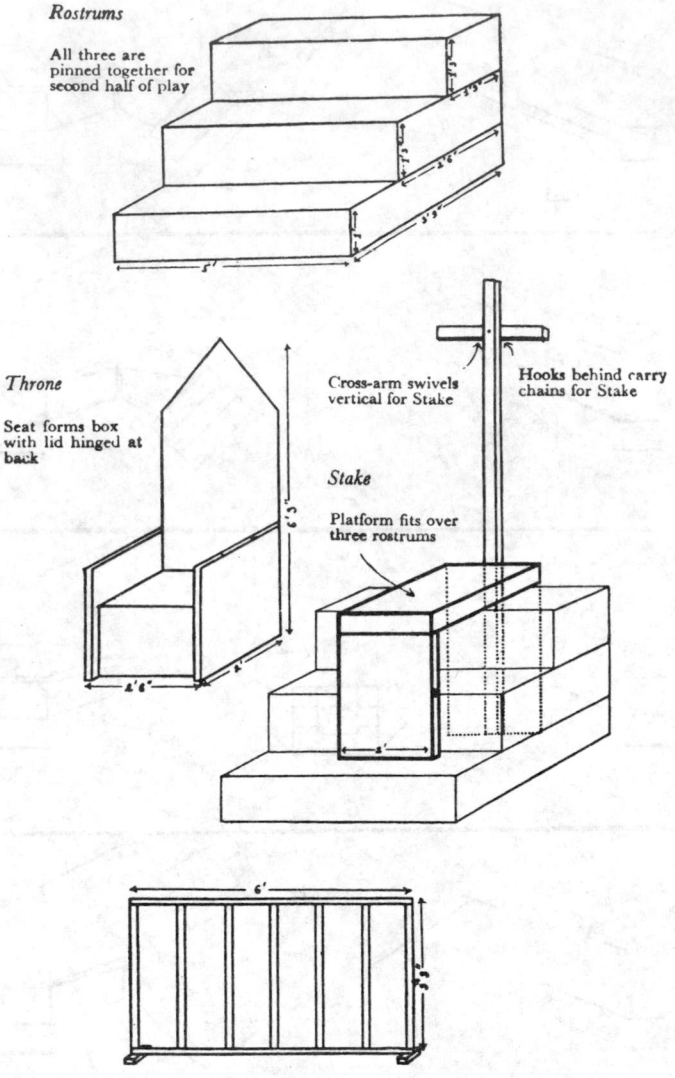

Rostrums

All three are pinned together for second half of play

Throne

Seat forms box with lid hinged at back

Cross-arm swivels vertical for Stake

Hooks behind carry chains for Stake

Stake

Platform fits over three rostrums

Fence